Venus
WITH BICEPS

David Chapman

2011

Seattle, Wa

Cover Illustration: The lovely lady in the ostrich-plumed hat who flexes her impressive biceps is Laverie Vallee, better known by her stage name of Charmion. She was a successful performer in circuses and vaudeville theaters, and starred in an early movie by Thomas Edison. Few women in the first decade of the twentieth century had such impressive musculature, and even fewer would dare to display it for the camera for fear of appearing too uppity and manly. As Charmion clearly shows, a woman can have muscles and still appear feminine. This photo is dated 1904; the photographer was Frederick Whitman Glasier. (From the collection of the John and Mable Ringling Museum of Art Archives.)

Venus
WITH BICEPS

A Pictorial History of Muscular Women

DAVID L. CHAPMAN & PATRICIA VERTINSKY

Arsenal Pulp Press | Vancouver

ARSENAL PULP PRESS
Suite 101, 211 East Georgia St.
Vancouver, BC
Canada V6A 1Z6
arsenalpulp.com

The publisher gratefully acknowledges the support of the Canada Council for the Arts and the British Columbia Arts Council for its publishing program, and the Government of Canada through the Canada Book Fund and the Government of British Columbia through the Book Publishing Tax Credit Program for its publishing activities.

Efforts have been made to locate copyright holders of source material wherever possible. The publisher welcomes hearing from any copyright holders of material used in this book who have not been contacted.

Front cover illustration, oritingally black & white (see page 2), is used courtesy of The John and Mable Ringling Museum of Art. Colorized by David Berryman.
Book design by Shyla Seller
Editing by Susan Safyan
All images courtesy of David L. Chapman; image restoration by David Berryman

Printed and bound in Hong Kong

Library and Archives Canada Cataloguing in Publication
Chapman, David L., 1948-
          Venus with biceps : a pictorial history of muscular
women / David L. Chapman with Patricia Vertinsky.

Includes bibliographical references and index.
Also available in electronic format.
ISBN 978-1-55152-370-5

          1. Women bodybuilders—History. 2. Women
bodybuilders—Pictorial works. I. Vertinsky, Patricia
Anne, 1942- II. Title.

HQ1219.C53 2010   306.4'613   C2010-902977-1

Contents

7 | Foreword

11 | Introduction

21 | Muscularity and the Female Body *Patricia Vertinsky*

47 | Foremothers

135 | Pumping Wood

195 | Pursuing the Healthy Life

233 | Wonder Women

293 | From Figure to Physique

347 | Conclusion: Let's Get Physical

357 | Index

Acknowledgments

In writing and assembling this book, I have been helped by many people. Michael Murphy of Westerly, Rhode Island, supplied both moral and material support throughout the process. Larry Aumann of Manitowoc, Wisconsin, assisted me continually with both photographs and encouragement. Laurie Fierstein of New York City was always ready with wise advice, factual clarification, and friendly support. One of the most important scholars of muscular women, Jan Todd of the University of Texas at Austin, gave me generous help and advice.

The greatest assistance came from my patient and long-suffering partner, David Berryman. He used his technological skills to turn many dim and tattered photographs into the wonderful images that appear in this book. I often handed him some scuffed and frayed illustration and asked, "Do you think you can make this look good?" He invariably could.

FOREWORD

David L. Chapman

Contemporary female bodybuilders tend to elicit pretty strong reactions; some of these responses are positive, but most range anywhere from disgust to incredulity. My own interest in female muscularity was inspired by two seminal events, the first of which occurred in California in 1987 and the second a dozen years later in New York City.

Muscle Beach was once one of the most important venues in Southern California for bodybuilding. The little strip of sand between Santa Monica Pier and Venice Beach was made famous in the 1940s and '50s by the gymnasts, acrobats, and high vaulting adagio dancers, who regularly put on free balancing and athletic shows for the public. It was a place you could go to on summer afternoons (and summer is a very long season in Los Angeles) and find superbly muscled athletes in brief attire practicing their jumps, handstands, and human pyramids there on the warm and forgiving sands. It was also one of the few places in the world, outside of a circus, where you could find muscular women—girls who had sculpted their physiques to a fare-thee-well by lifting weights or supporting partners on their generous deltoids—female athletes like Relna Brewer, Paula Unger, and (most wonderful of all, to me) Abbye Stockton, known to her friends as "Pudgy."

Unfortunately, the seaside idyll at Muscle Beach ended after sex scandals, sleazy conduct, and a general distrust of athletes and the people they attracted caused the area to be closed down starting late in 1958. Almost thirty years after closing it down, the city of Santa Monica agreed to put up a sign marking the site of the old Muscle Beach. Since expensive beachfront properties had now sanitized the neighborhood, the city organized a commemoration of the beach's former glory, and invited a number of the old denizens back to celebrate

David L. Chapman and Abbye "Pudgy" Stockton, Muscle Beach, California, 1988.

the erection of the historical marker. I got word that the celebration would take place and was determined to go so that I could meet some of the old-time bodybuilders whom I had long admired. At the time, I was a writer for a couple of bodybuilding magazines, so it wasn't hard to finagle an invitation.

At the event, I was not disappointed; there were many stars in attendance whom I was happy to meet. The greatest thrill of the day came when I encountered a beautiful and elegantly muscular woman who had acquired the undeserved nickname of "Pudgy." I was particularly thrilled to meet her because of the role that she had played in the history of bodybuilding, especially women's. Pudgy led the way. For many years, the diminutive lady with whom I was merrily chatting at Muscle Beach had been one of the few brave enough to buck the trend against strongly muscled women. Her photos in *Strength and Health* (the premiere fitness magazine of the 1940s and '50s) and other periodicals proved conclusively that exercising with weights would not make a woman "overly" muscular or mannish.

After talking with Pudgy, I happened to see another unmistakable and highly original character who'd played a part in both the fitness revolution and women's exercise: Jack LaLanne. There he was, right in front of me, an animated and obviously fit little man offering opinions, clowning around, and generally having a great time at the center of a group of admirers. I had known of him since the 1950s when my mother religiously watched his mid-morning exercise program on television. It was largely thanks to LaLanne that women all over North America learned the rudiments of fitness and good eating habits. My mother was something of an exercise fanatic, and she would never dream of missing his show. She had somewhat mixed opinions on Jack's nutritional advice, and she agreed with almost everyone that he was eccentric in his speech and behavior, but she still loved him.

My interest in muscular women received another impetus in the year 2000 when the New Museum of Contemporary Art in New York mounted an extraordinary exhibition of modern and vintage art related to strongwomen called "Picturing the Modern Amazon," which was something of a turning point in the study of female bodybuilders. Prior to the show, I met an extraordinary woman named Laurie Fierstein, who was one of the curators of the exhibition. She was both a physique athlete of magnificent proportions and an eloquent and intelligent historian who helped me to understand the meaning and importance of female bodybuilders. Laurie looked at my collection of photographs and chose several items for the show. Later, I was invited to give a lecture at the Museum on the iconography of strong women in historical images.

Laurie Fierstein, photo courtesy www. WPWMagazineOnline.com

This was the first time that I had the opportunity to meet and talk with women who had honed their physiques to an unprecedented size and mass. I found most of them to be pleasant company, confident (but aware of their faults), and enthusiastic, but not aggressive. In short, they were pretty normal for athletes at the upper end of their chosen field. I wanted to know why they spent hours in the gym building bodies that most people (men and women) found unattractive. The answer was almost always the same: they did it for themselves. Building muscles made them feel better about themselves. According to Leslie Heywood in her excellent book *Bodymakers*, most contemporary women bodybuilders don't care if we like the way they look or not. They aren't building their bodies for us, anyway. The question is not whether they are sexually appealing for others but whether they excel at what they do for themselves. In the end, it is an issue of self-fulfillment. It was a simple explanation, but it made me wonder about the women who had tried to build their bodies in previous generations. Did they worry about gender-identity issues a hundred or more years ago? Did these muscular females agonize over their mesomorphic genes and their need to express themselves? Who can answer these questions? All I know for sure is that, then as now, they were individuals who chose to be themselves regardless of what others thought or said, and as such they expanded and redefined femininity itself.

I have been collecting images of muscular women for nigh on to thirty years, and the results of this collecting mania are found in the present book. All the images in this volume come from my own collection, which I have accumulated over several decades. Consequently, this cannot be a definitive record of female muscularity; it is derived from the opportunities I had to acquire these images and my own personal tastes. I have attempted, however, to be as comprehensive and systematic as possible in choosing the images and writing the text.

Sheena comic book panel (1942).

INTRODUCTION

David L. Chapman

There is something profoundly upsetting about a proud, confident, unrepentantly muscular woman. She risks being seen by her viewers as dangerous, alluring, odd, beautiful or, at worst, a sort of raree show. She is, in fact, a smorgasbord of mixed messages. This inability to come to grips with a strong, heavily muscled woman accounts for much of the confusion and downright hostility that often greets her. *Venus With Biceps* traces the images of such women during the almost 200 years between 1800 and 1980. It was a formative period in both the history of female strength and of popular reaction to it; at the beginning of the era, the first strongwomen appeared on the variety-show stages of Europe. By 1980, the first Ms. Olympia bodybuilding contest was held, thus marking the start of a new and different epoch in female muscularity.

It is quite common today for women to go to the gym, exercise, lift weights, and (sometimes) cultivate their muscles in a way that would have been unusual just a generation ago. With the advent of steroids, hormones, supplements, and other artificial growth stimulants, the possibilities for female muscularity have multiplied exponentially, and as female bodies transform themselves into something bigger, bolder, and different from what had been idealized in the past, the same old uncertainties and sexual ambiguities keep society bubbling away with loud but hardly new controversies.

Theorists of body structure have divided humans into three types: the endomorph, or the soft, fleshy, belly-centered person; the ectomorph, or the lean, brain-centered individual; and the mesomorph, the athletic muscle-centered person. According to this schema, we are all mixtures of these three types, but sometimes a single type predominates, and if one is in the latter group, he or she will sprout muscles faster than the rest of us. But is this a boon or a curse for female mesomorphs?

Extraordinarily strong men and women have always existed (though verifiable evidence of their existence prior to the nineteenth century is rare), and some forms of strength athletics date from ancient times. But bodybuilding as a distinctive activity matured in the modern world. There were a few muscular anomalies in earlier times, largely relegated to the world of myth and legend (e.g., Hercules, Paul Bunyan). Like most other sports, muscle building was born in the Industrial Age when the techniques, the leisure time, and the will to get out and do something about one's physical condition all coalesced. Sports, as we know them, were invented in England, the first nation to industrialize. In an age when machines were stronger and more efficient than their human operators, it became necessary to take the measure of one's peers in another way, and for many physically minded people, athletic competition was the answer—at least, for men. But were sporting contests appropriate for ladies?

Some nineteenth-century moralists saw female athletics as the first step on the road to moral degradation. In an 1878 article in *The American Christian Review*, author J.R. Headington argued that women's participation in sport could set susceptible females down a nine-step path to sin and humiliation. For example, he theorized, a simple croquet party could lead to picnics, picnics led to dances, dances led to absence from church, absence from church led to immoral conduct, immoral conduct led to exclusion from church, exclusion from church led to running away, running away led to poverty and discontent, poverty and discontent led to shame and disgrace, and shame and disgrace led to ruin. It was apparently a short and slippery slope from knocking a croquet ball with a wooden mallet to a life of humiliation and prostitution. In the face of such disapproval, it was little wonder that many women were deeply conflicted on the subject of physical culture.

After the passage of several years and much soul-searching, most arbiters of social correctness agreed that some physical exercise was good for women, but it had to be gentle and non-competitive. Fitness and health were fine so long as one did not take them too far. Calisthenics, rhythmical drills, and dancing were all judged as suitable for young ladies, but God forbid a girl should want to play baseball, football, or (worst of all) lift weights. Thus a debate began which has never been completely resolved: should females strive to develop their muscles as avidly as males? Should a woman attempt to cross over into that dark other-world of hyper-muscularity? What might she look like and, more importantly, what might she act like after her sinews had been honed and hardened? It was a question that threw many nineteenth- and twentieth-century authorities into tizzies of fear, outrage, and consternation. "Nothing," as expert female strength historian Al Thomas confirmed, "scares the stalwarts of our culture and church and state nearly so resoundingly as even the most gentle-hearted and kindly disposed female mesomorph."

One of the battlefields of this conflict appeared in popular imagery. Posters, magazine illustrations, comic books, and most particularly, photography offered an outlet of expression for many muscular women. In the early days, however, powerful women were packaged for the general public in a limited number of ways. They were portrayed variously as sexless mannequins, voluptuous love goddesses, stern but sexy dominatrices, circus sideshow freaks, male-hating viragos, wacky health nuts, or any number of other roles—almost anything except what they really were: physically commanding, mentally balanced, athletic women.

Photographs and other images of stoutly muscled women from before 1980 are not nearly as common as images of male athletes, and there are several reasons for this scarcity. First, women could not properly appear with bare upper torsos as could the men. The occasional naked shoulders and backs that appeared in some photos were considered very daring. Form-fitting attire, such as the tights worn by vaudeville strongwomen and acrobats, was much too exciting for many Edwardian social critics. The most famous case in point occurred in 1905 when the publisher of *Physical Culture* magazine, Bernarr Macfadden, organized a women's physique contest at New York's Madison Square Garden. Posters advertising the competition featuring a photo of a young lady wearing long underwear were put up all over the city. When New York's Society for the Suppression of Vice saw the posters, they immediately declared them to be obscene and had Macfadden arrested. Unfortunately, vice was not suppressed by this action—just the opposite occurred. Thanks to the unwitting and free publicity, the contest was a huge success; still, it pointed out the dangers of female physique display.

A second reason for the rarity of photographic representations of female muscularity was the fear that a well-developed musculature could unsex a woman. Until the middle of the twentieth century, it was generally considered dangerous and unhealthy for women to build muscles. If a woman began to become muscular, it was thought that she could lose her health, femininity, and (very possibly) her husband. Besides, popular wisdom decreed that decent women were better off getting their exercise by doing household chores rather than messing about with dumbbells and Indian clubs.

A third explanation was that viewers were simply not ready to "see" muscles on a woman. Mesomorphic women had existed since the dawn of human history, but astonishingly few people seem to have realized this. It is no accident that there are no classical representations of strong, muscular women; there are, for instance, no corresponding female statues to match the Farnese Hercules. Such bodies were not recognized as valid. No one (or very few people) thought to ask a woman to flex her biceps because no one—sometimes not even the possessors of the biceps—realized that they were there. Even superbly strong women were often reluctant to display their muscular attributes in photographs, opting for "glamour" shots rather than real physique photos.

A woman's physical malleability was considered unique to her gender because many observers viewed the female body as being more susceptible to trends and fads. So when a woman posed for the camera, she had a variety of acceptable poses that she could assume. She could look hard or soft; she could hide or hint at her muscles. An athletic girl could imitate Venus or Diana; she could be alluring, fearsome, or graceful; she could look stern or compassionate, and all the while her male spectators could project their own fantasies on her. Fashions in dress and hairstyle changed, so why not bodies too? Women could diet and exercise until they achieved a perfect form, but a paragon of female beauty could also be compressed into an acceptable form by artificial means. Starting in the seventeenth century, women had deformed their torsos by squeezing them into various shapes with tightly laced corsets. By the end of the nineteenth century, the hourglass shape was in vogue. A few decades later, the "S" shape (bosoms pushed forward and buttocks thrust back) became popular. Developing muscularity was therefore seen as just one of many ways that a female could shift and redefine her appearance. It would take several more decades before women were freed from the corset, and a principal reason was the advancement of sport. One of the results of this change was that vigorous and healthy females became more common in popular imagery.

The images might have been more common, but they were not really more original in scope or design; in fact, there were only four basic methods of presentation for muscular women. One of the most common ways of presenting a strongwoman was to portray her demonstrating her strength, but in non-threatening ways. There are therefore many pictures of female athletes placidly smiling and showing very little effort as they hoist barbells, anvils, or husbands into the air; while sometimes this was the result of trick photography, sometimes it was not, revealing the subject's very real strength.

A second type of typical image of strongwomen is the "living statue" pose. Often the model would be placed against a column or posed as a famous sculpture from the classical past. This was also an excellent way to avoid censorship since one could always claim that the model was merely imitating the ancients to inform the moderns. In none of the living-statue photos, however, were any muscles flexed or feats performed, as this would have been unseemly and threatening to many male viewers.

Another solution to the problem of displaying provocative female bodies without affronting nervous censors was the "fitness" or "exercise" photo. Ladies could demonstrate exercise techniques and perform other educational services. The usual attire for such images was a leotard or tights of some sort, and we may be sure that many male viewers were not looking at the photos for a few tips in performing leg dips. As the nudism movement picked up adherents in the late 1920s, women began to be comfortable wearing less clothing while exercising. Some athletic females appeared completely naked.

The final and rarest way that early image makers portrayed physically impressive women was what we would today recognize as the true physique picture in which the women were posed specifically to show off their musculature. And yet, flexing arms to show off bicep development was something that even the strongest female athletes were reluctant to do. Such images would show that the women had apparently lost their traditional femininity because they had built powerful muscles, sometimes as big as men's. This was simply too much for many males (and more than a few females) to countenance.

One of the most curious aspects of this whole phenomenon of muscular women is that there are many images and magazine reports of muscular women from the period of 1900 to 1914, but after that, it becomes increasingly difficult to find proudly muscular females in the books and periodicals of the time (until the late 1970s). There are perhaps several reasons for the great abundance and variety of images of muscular women before World War I. Fairs, circuses, and vaudeville stages provided a convenient venue for strongwomen, but as films and other new forms of entertainment spread, these old forms gradually disappeared. In addition, many variety theaters shut down or reduced their shows during the war; this was especially true in Central Europe. When vaudeville declined, images of the performers became rare.

Pictures of strongwomen may also have been more abundant before 1914 because they had considerable curiosity value. Images of pretty showgirls in pink tights and ruffles were easy to come by; they could be found in just about every issue of *The Police Gazette* or on many of the illustrated cards that were tucked into packages of tobacco, but strongwomen offered a new and slightly daring form of the ideal female body. Perhaps this is because illustrations of muscular women in form-hugging stage costumes offered men a different means to ogle the female form at a time when most burlesque girls were posed as sweet and simpering love toys. Male admirers might claim that they were merely studying the subject's perky pectorals, not leering at her upturned bosom. Paradoxically, as female athletes became more common, they lost their value as oddities. After some initial confusion, most men apparently chose to look at less formidably developed female forms. Despite this gradual decline of interest, the strongwoman remained an unusual but reliable ingredient in the menu of Edwardian eroticism.

Part of the reason images of strongwomen were limited and misunderstood stems from the deep confusion about what a female bodybuilder really was. Were women who trained their muscles to perfection and then displayed them on a posing dais really that far from the beauty pageant contestants who paraded their gorgeous selves on a stage? Was a muscular woman still "feminine"? Were developed muscles the exclusive domain of men, or could women sport biceps, too? This confusion led to many absurd situations, not the least of which are the photos that appeared in the 1950s and 1970s showing women working out with weights wearing leotards, jewelry, big hair, heavy makeup, and stiletto heels. It appears is as if they were desperately afraid that their femininity and desirability would be called into question if they were shown in normal workout gear. Many of these models were also very careful to have themselves photographed with light weights or tiny dumbbells.

Artists and photographers were not the only ones confused about the muscular women whose images they recorded; the women themselves were sometimes unclear on what they were doing. This confusion often resulted in isolating female strength athletes from the mainstream of athletes and society in general. It is true that a few women made careers out of their beauty and their muscularity, but they were never perceived of as part of a cohesive sport; they were almost always seen as bizarre anomalies. Although it was there in front of them, both men and women refused to see the muscularity that was in plain sight. Part of the reason for this blindness was that many women were encouraged to conceal their own muscular physiques. Aside from a few professional strongwomen who lifted weights and demonstrated their skill at strength sports on the vaudeville stage, the only women who dared to display their physical development were circus acrobats and trapeze artists. Hundreds of photos showing female acrobats flexing demurely behind a circus wagon were made in the early to mid-twentieth century, and these have become valuable icons of a hidden world of women's strength.

North American women were not the only ones who did not know quite what to make of a girl with biceps and washboard abs. As late as 1937, French physical culturists were warning females against the pernicious effects of sport and excessive exercise: "Girls and adolescents," warned one authority, "leave violent games to the men; if you run fast or if you feel stronger than your friends, do not take advantage of them. Try to remain feminine; you will never be men." Women were advised to seek "harmonious and rounded figures" and to adhere to such graceful occupations as rhythmic gymnastics. "Forget running and the high jump, avoid the games of football or rugby, and suppress the desire to be the strongest in your muscles or your endurance." Women were encouraged to compete in the areas of grace and beauty, but never to "deform" their bodies and faces by "exaggerated effort."

After the end of World War II, when information began to flow across the Atlantic once more, Europeans were rather surprised to learn that, in the intervening years, American and Canadian male bodybuilders had become bigger and more muscular than their counterparts from across the Atlantic. European strongmen and women gradually realized that if they wished to compete on an international scale, they had to adopt the new techniques and nutritional habits of their cousins across the sea. These innovations included a high-protein, low-carbohydrate diet, and dramatically intense workouts that increased muscle mass more efficiently than ever before. The revelations also caused them to start seeing the female form in a new way. Perhaps, they reasoned, there was not simply one ideal to fit all women, and articles began to appear that explored beauties representing all three types of the feminine form: the Venus (tall, ample breasts, narrow waist and hips); the Callipygian (short, hips wider than the breasts); and the Diana (V-shaped upper body). Of these three, the Venus type was greatly preferred, but by admitting that other body types might also be valid, the door opened to other models.

Until surprisingly recently, it did not matter whether one were a Venus, Cal-lipygian, or Diana or even mesomorphic in shape—the most important thing was that a woman display herself in an appropriately feminine way. Even such veteran weight-trainers as Pudgy Stockton posed to show grace and form, not muscularity (although her muscular bulk is clearly there in the photos). It was not until the mid-1970s that women slowly began to show off their muscles in traditionally male-only bodybuilding poses. There are plenty of images of women who want to slim down or firm up their figures, and they are perfectly willing to use weight training to do so, but beyond that they do not go. Women with hefty, well-built physiques were certainly out there, but they were not showing themselves to photographers as such. Ironically, as the world was con-vulsing into waves of liberation movements, many athletic women were still reluctant to show themselves as powerful, independent, and muscular. All that would change in the 1980s.

Muscularity in women can clearly be seen as emblematic of their psychologi-cal and political strength, yet women's bodybuilding did not become popular until the late 1970s. Despite the burgeoning of the Women's Liberation move-ment in the late 1960s, many women were afraid to break out of the sexual ste-reotypes that had been imposed on them by a society dominated by traditional-ist men. Until almost 1980, most women were simply not ready to relinquish the physical stereotypes of grace, beauty, and frailty that had served (and con-strained) them for so long. A woman couldn't "get a husband" if she had bigger biceps than he did. Unfortunately, male chauvinist pigs were not the only ones who lobbed cruel arrows at muscular women.

Feminists of a certain stripe have also been deeply mistrustful of overly strong, firmly developed women. They often harbor suspicions that female bodybuilders are either beauty queens in disguise or that women physique ath-letes are simply trying to become alternate and inferior versions of men. This is a controversy that has remained to the present day and has never been fully resolved, and it isn't likely to as long as the motives of physique building are questioned. Naturally, women begin to work out for a variety of reasons, but one of the driving forces is to achieve mastery over one's own body. A beauty contestant is thought to be someone who has surrendered to male values; a physique contender, on the other hand, is seen to make her own values and dare us to accept her as she is and as she wants to be. If nothing else, we have to admire her *chutzpah*.

Physically powerful and heavily muscled women have always been upsetting to the status quo because they reversed the "natural" dominance of the male. Historian Al Thomas noted that many insecure men feared that, "the bigger the body, the bigger the threat." Here were women who sported muscles as large and impressive as those of men. It was not a coincidence that muscular females came onto the scene at the same time that women were beginning to flex their political and social muscles, too. The images of some women in this book might look harmless and faintly ridiculous today, but in their day these pictures and the women who posed for them were considered threats to the masculine system of supremacy.

Many of the same battles that were being fought over a century ago are still being waged today. When we see pictures of women bodybuilders, it is all too easy to dismiss them as freaks, lesbian man-haters, or steroid abusers—after all, labels are so much easier to deal with than realities.

Bibliography

Addison, Heather. *Hollywood and the Rise of Physical Culture*. New York: Routledge, 2003.

Anonymous. "Les Américains et les Canadiens veulent des athlètes de grand formats, puissants et musclés." *La Culture Physique*, 51 no. 636 (January 1947): 9.

Anonymous. "The New Ideal of Beauty" *Time Magazine*, Monday, August 30, 1982.

Banner, Lois W. *American Beauty*. New York: Knopf, 1983.

De Bizerte, P., "Le sport moderne transforme-t-il les femmes en homes?" *La Culture Physique*, 44 no. 569 (September 1937): 283.

Desbonnet, Edmond. *Les rois de la force: Histoire de tous les hommes forts depuis les temps anciens jusqu'à nos jours*. Paris: Berger-Levrault/Librairie Athlétique, 1911.

Frueh, Joanna, Laurie Fierstein, and Judith Stein. *Picturing the Modern Amazon*. New York: Rizzoli International Publications, 2000.

Gori, Gigliola. *Italian Fascism and the Female Body: Sport, Submissive Women and Strong Mothers*. London: Routledge, 2004.

Groth, Lothar. *Die starken Männer: Eine Geschichte der Kraftakrobatik*. Berlin: Henschelverlag, 1985.

Haerdle, Stephanie. *Keine Angst haben, das ist unser Beruf! Kunstreiterinnen, Dompteusen und andere Zirkusartistinnen*. Berlin: AvivA Verlag, 2007.

Heywood, Leslie. *Bodymakers: A Cultural Anatomy of Women's Body Building*. New Brunswick, NJ: Rutgers University Press, 1998.

Marwick, Arthur. *Beauty in History: Society, Politics and Personal Appearance c. 1500 to the present*. New York: Thames and Hudson, 1988.

Thesander, Marianne. *The Feminine Ideal*. London: Reaktion Books Ltd., 1997.

Thomas, Al and others. *The Female Physique Athlete: A History to Date 1977–1983*. Midland Park, NJ: Abs-solutely/The Women's Physique Publication, 1983.

Todd, Jan. "The Origins of Weight Training for Female Athletes in North America," *Iron Game History*, 2 no. 2 (April 1992): 4–14.

———. *Physical Culture and the Body Beautiful: Purposive Exercise in the Lives of American Women 1800–1875*. Macon, GA: Mercer University Press, 1998.

MUSCULARITY AND THE FEMALE BODY

Patricia Vertinsky

This book is a celebration of the strong female body, its vivid images designed to disrupt the traditional equation of men with strength and women with weakness. Although muscularity has long been used to connote masculine beauty and male power and strength, the historical record shows that numerous women have defied traditional conventions by flexing their muscles and displaying their strength for enjoyment, remuneration, and the display of personal agency and professional power. Yet their opportunities have all too often been restricted by scientific and medical theories that have labeled them the weaker sex and by social pressures to labor for beauty rather than a strong and powerful body—this despite the demands of motherhood and onerous domestic duties. Indeed, historians have struggled to show how complex, contradictory, and controlling has been the advice meted out to women about how to be beautiful but also useful, dainty but strong, slender and rounded, modest yet erotic. The overt display of female musculature, however, and the invitation to the viewer to admire, and perhaps desire, a strong female body reminds us that the muscle gap has never been carved in stone. The kaleidoscope of strong female figures on the stage, in the circus, on the pages of advice books, outdoors, and in the gym reveals a determination to challenge the order of things, to stare back at the objectifying gaze, refashion femininity, and add a voice to feminist struggles for equality and self-realization.

The Ambivalence of Female Muscularity

When the bodybuilding Mecca, Gold's Gym, first opened in California in 1964 for hardcore male bodybuilders, one of its members was heard to describe the gym's space as "ovary free."[1] His meaning was clear. Women were not expected to be seen working out in an arena where the building of muscle was the focus of activity as they would be transgressing the norms of what is considered "natural" for the female body. "We always knew women could never build muscles, at least not, uh, real women," wrote the author of a *Sports Illustrated* article a decade and a half later.[2] Yet muscularity is just as much a product of cultural practices as it is of biological possibilities. Being a woman—or a man—is not reducible to internal organs, size, shape, or chromosomes. Social, historical, political, and economic forces shape who we are and how we perceive our gender identities in addition to our biology. Indeed, the very idea of the "natural" body is a mythology, though it has been clung to and reproduced, especially in contexts where the biological is used as an explanation for cultural inequalities and discrimination. In spite of evidence to the contrary, women have historically been considered close to nature, and over the years their bodies have become the properties of science and medicine, tied to the idea of a fixed natural state whose sporting and exercising activities have been understood in terms of causal biological explanations. The female body has been imbued with a nurturing, maternal, and passive character, an identification with "femininity" that all too often has been used to restrict women's cultural roles. In "The Real Truth about the Female Body," Barbara Ehrenreich and Barbara Maddux point out that "'female still tends to connote the oozing, bleeding, swelling, hot-flashing, swamp-creature side of the species, its tiny brain marinating in the primal hormonal broth." Biology, they continue, "has usually been only too glad to claim the human female as its slave."[3]

The ambivalence about women and muscularity has a long history, as it pushes at the limits of gender identity. Images of muscular women are disconcerting, even threatening. They disrupt the equation of men with strength and women with weakness that underpins gender roles and power relations. In fact, the female muscled body is so dangerous, say Alan Mansfield and Barbara Mc-

---

1   Alan. M. Klein, "Pumping Iron," *Society* 22, no. 6 (1985): 69.

2   David Levin, "Here She Is, Miss, Well, What?," *Sports Illustrated,* March 17, 1980, 66.

3   Barbara Ehrenreich and Barbara Maddux, "The Real Truth about the Female Body," *Time* (1999), http://www.time.com/time/printout/0,8816,990379,00.html.

Ginn, "that the proclamation of gender must be made very loudly indeed."[4] The media furor over the powerful physique and distinctly muscular appearance of Caster Semanya, the South African who won the women's 800 meters final at the 2009 Track and Field World championships in Berlin, pointed to the not-so-subtle gender bias of western standards of appearance. Even where today's female bodybuilders resist the controlling discipline of femininity, they often seek to produce feminized bodies of a different kind that are equally imprinted with the gendered meanings of culture.[5] In her feminist analysis of the ways in which feminine bodies are produced in western societies, Sandra Lee Bartky points out how technologies of disciplinary power act to enlist women into becoming self-policing subjects, working to produce bodies of the right size and shape with the "appropriate" feminine posture, gestures, and movements, with "suitable" surface ornamentation and display.[6] For females, it's not what you do, it's how you look while doing it. If women in bodybuilding follow the same growth curve over time as have the men, suggests photographer Bill Dobbins, "we will see female competitors much bigger, hard, denser, more muscular and more defined ... but they will still be shapely, symmetrical and proportioned. They will have wide shoulders and a small waist. Their muscles will be full and taper down to small joints. The best will combine beauty of physique with overall aesthetics, including beautiful faces."[7]

Caster Semanya.

Muscles and Power: Advantage Male

Clearly, it is important to study the body in relation to questions of power, and according to Richard Dyer, muscles are the sign of male power.[8] Muscles

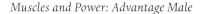

4   Alan Mansfield and Barbara McGinn, "Pumping Irony: The Muscular and the Feminine," in *Body Matters: Essays on the Sociology of the Body*, ed. S. Scott and D. Morgan (London: Falmer, 1993).

5   Susan Bordo, "Reading the Slender Body," in *Body/Politics: Women and the Discourses of Science,* ed. M. Jacobus, E. Fox Keller, and S. Shuttleworth (New York: Routledge, 1990).

6   Sandra Lee Bartky, "Foucault, Femininity and the Modernization of Patriarchal Power," in *Feminism and Foucault, Reflections on Resistance*, ed. I. Diamond and L. Quinby (Boston, MA: Northeastern University Press, 1988).

7   Bill Dobbins, "Female Muscle: What's It About; How I Photograph It," The Bill Dobbins Female Physique Art Gallery, http://www.billdobbins.net/PUBLIC/pages/femuscle.htm.

8   Christine Anne Holmlund, "Visible Differences and Flex Appeal: The Body, Sex, Sexuality and Race in the 'Pumping Iron' Films," in *Out of Bounds: Sport, Media and the Politics of Identity,* ed. A. Baker and T. Boyd (Bloomington and Indianapolis: Indiana

have been viewed as a key fundamental biological difference between men and women and are therefore invested with binary meanings that negate passivity, softness, weakness, and homosexuality. Part of learning to be male, says Raewyn Connell in her analysis of masculinities, is learning to cultivate a body that speaks of power, competence, and domination.[9] Indeed, "the body as presented and interpreted in terms of its muscular development has been restricted almost exclusively to the male body."[10] Men are expected to act, women to appear.[11] Thus women have simply not been able to develop and use their muscular bodies to accrue the kind of social, cultural, and economic capital that the "Governator" of California, Arnold Schwarzenegger, for example, has accumulated in his celebrated career. Where Schwarzenegger's imagery straddles physical culture, Hollywood movies, and American politics, his images provide a keen insight into the symbolic power of muscle in those arenas that continue to be male-dominated and in which muscular male bodies are signifiers of personal and political power.[12] Arnold's body, a walking billboard of invulnerability, was constructed/educated (in his own view) to stand for his ability to "fill up the space of the world."[13]

Commentators have linked this cult of the muscular male body to the rise of the sport and celebrity industry in modern society, though the distinct articulation of muscles with masculinity can be viewed as a much longer historical and cultural process.[14] As early as the ancient Greeks, muscles signified masculine beauty, male strength, and power.[15] In his brilliant comparison of

---

University Press, 1997); Richard Dyer, "The White Man's Muscles," in *The Masculinity Studies Reader*, ed. R. Adams and D. Savran (Oxford: Blackwell Publishers, 2002).

9   R.W. Connell, *Masculinities* (NSW, Australia: Allen & Unwin, 2005).

10   Kenneth. R. Dutton, *The Perfectible Body: The Western Ideal of Male Physical Development* (New York: Continuum, 1995), 13.

11   John Berger, *"Ways of Seeing": Based on the BBC Television Series* (London: Penguin Group, 1972), 47.

12   Ellexis Boyle, "The Intertextual Terminator: The Role of Film in Branding Arnold Schwarzenegger," Journal of Communication Inquiry 34, no. 1 (2010): 42–60.

13   Arnold Schwarzenegger, *Arnold: The Education of a Bodybuilder* (New York: Simon and Schuster, 1977).

14   D. Magill, "Spectacular Male Bodies and Jazz Age Celebrity Culture," In *Framing Celebrity: New Directions in Celebrity Culture*, ed. S. Holmes and S. Redmond (London and New York: Routledge, 2006).

15   Dutton, *The Perfectible Body*.

diverse medical traditions Shigehisa Kuriyama shows how muscularity was a peculiarly Western preoccupation resulting from particular ways of thinking about, touching, seeing, and being a body. Interest in individual muscles, and indeed the very notion of muscles, developed uniquely in medical traditions rooted in ancient Greece. Elsewhere, as in China, for example, ignorance of musculature was the rule.[16]

Kuriyama reminds us that Greek muscle-consciousness was intimately related to notions of power and individual agency. According to Greek physician Galen, muscles allow us to choose what we do, and when and how; and this choice marks the divide between voluntary actions and involuntary processes.[17] At the same time, modern western societies have tended to follow the tastes of ancient Greece in the status accorded to male athletic muscularity as an aesthetic ideal (including eroticism), and present intuitions about human muscularity owe much to the history of western art. A body without muscles, said fifteenth-century artist Leone Battista Alberti, was like clothes without the person.[18] Art historian George Hersey takes a particular vantage point focused on sexual selection to show how art has given rise to normative body types that link physiological drives to aesthetic impulses. He demonstrates how, long ago, Greek sculptors Polykleitos and Praxiteles created human proportional systems based on numbers and their rational sequences and symmetries that were believed to contain innate moral powers. Their systems (which in a sense meant that beauty was dependent on its numerical analysis) have been repeated down the ages, contributing to nineteenth- and twentieth-century racial science, physical anthropology, and preferences for dominating male mesomorphic physiques and soft, curved, cello shapes for women.[19]

The Greek Slave by Hiram Powers.

16 Shigehisa Kuriyama, *The Expressiveness of the Body and the Divergence of Greek and Chinese Medicine* (New York: Zone Books, 1999), 111.

17 Galen, Peri myōn kinêsiōs 1.1. (K 4.367) quoted in Kuriyama, *The Expressiveness of the Body,* 144.

18 Leone Battista Alberti, De Statue, 1450s, quoted in Kuriyama, *The Expressiveness of the Body,* 116.

19 George Hersey, *The Evolution of Allure. Sexual Selection from the Medici Venus to the Incredible Hunk* (Cambridge, MA: MIT Press, 1996), 44–47. For centuries, the Farnese Hercules exemplified the Polykleitan muscular extreme and today's bodybuilders often strike the pose of this statue, 168.

Muscles, Morals and Mind: Learning to Read the Body from the Outside In
Craniometry, phrenology, physiognomy, and comparative anatomy all shared long-standing beliefs that the outer body was a window into a host of moral, temperamental, racial, or gender characteristics. Phrenologist Orson Squire Fowler placed a special interest on female bodies, believing that physical exercise and its concomitant muscular enlargement would enhance brain size and improve intellectual function—just like a fertilizer. Good muscles are more useful than anything, he said, working against the popular notion that the body's energy was a limited resource and that vigorous exercise would place too great demands upon the female body. Soft hands, he was sure, belonged to soft brains and soft and weak intellects.[20] Rather tellingly, his measure of the perfect female form belonged to Hiram Power's statue, the Greek Slave. "It shows large breasts, thighs, calves and arms … with a perfect proportion to all of them."[21]

As the science of measuring male and female human bodies and quantifying their functions matured during the nineteenth century, anthropometry became one more of a long line of sciences concerned with detailed measuring, comparing, and interpreting variability in parts of the body. Those favoring anthropometric techniques focused upon rigid standardized methods and quantifiable results, holding them out as objective and unambiguous. In particular, the proliferation of the photographic image provided a powerful tool to scientists measuring bodies in an attempt to identify criminals and prostitutes, illustrate scientific laws, and document medical procedures.[22] In many respects, however, in tying together physique and character (and encouraging certain physiques to be equated with superior mental and spiritual qualities), these an-

---

20 Orson Squire Fowler, *Phrenology and Physiology Explained and Applied to Education, and Self Improvement: Including the Intellectual and Moral Education and Government of Children* (New York: O.S. and L.N. Fowler, 1842), 22.

21 Orson Squire Fowler, *Private Lectures on Perfect Men, Women and Children, in Happy Families* (Sharon Station, NY: Mrs. O.S. Fowler, 1883).

22 Lorraine Anne Davis, "Investing in Photography," in *Cultures of Economics—Economics of Culture*, ed. Jackson Lears and Jens Van Scherpenberg (Heidelberg Universitats Winter, 2004). The nineteenth century put extraordinary faith in science's capacity to unravel the mysteries of the human body as well as having high expectations of photography. By mid-century, every British criminal was being photographed—a measure seen as a useful safeguard against crime since none could escape its crucial observation. William A. Ewing, *The Body Photographs of the Human Form* (New York: Chronicle Books, 2004), 18–19.

thropometric techniques had the reverse effect by reinforcing previously held beliefs about class, race, and gender.[23]

The Atlas of Men *and the (Never Published)* Atlas of Women

Among the early twentieth-century body prescribers that art historian Hersey discusses was psychologist William Sheldon, who was inspired by the work of Italian criminologist Cesare Lombroso, German psychiatrist Ernst Kretschmer, and Harvard anthropologist Ernest Hooton to continue the Renaissance and baroque practice of equating the body's features, proportions, and measurement with temperament and intellect. (Lombroso, for example, had noted that women's bodies were marked by traces of youth and the past: prehensile feet, left-handedness, dullness of the senses, and a resistance to pain.) In developing his somatotyping taxonomy dividing mankind into ectomorphs (thin), mesomorphs (muscular), and endomorphs (fat), Sheldon placed his trust upon the surface of the body, unwilling to allow the eye to lose its longstanding diagnostic power to Freud and the ear.[24] His views—illustrated in *Varieties of Human Physique* (1940), *Varieties of Human Temperament* (1942), and *The Atlas of Men* (1954), that physique was destiny and that male mesomorphs should rule the world went well beyond the bounds of common sense, yet his projects were funded by the Rockefeller Foundation and adopted by those in higher education, especially physical education departments, for decades.[25]

Sheldon always planned an *Atlas of Women* as a companion to *The Atlas of Men*, which contained 1,175 carefully posed photographs of nearly nude white college men viewed from back, front, and side and from which the athletic muscular body emerges as the most heroic, biologically superior type.[26] Thousands of nude photographs of Ivy League college women had been collected by his

---

23 See Patricia Vertinsky, "Embodying Normalcy: Anthropometry and the Long Arm of William Sheldon's Somatotyping Project," *Journal of Sport History* 29, no. 1 (2002): 95–133. It should be noted that the perfect body in Western culture was only sustained and made imaginable by the imperfect body of the racial "other."

24 Vertinsky, "Embodying Normalcy."

25 "They are well able," he said "to command the environments their bodies so forcefully occupy." William H. Sheldon, and S.S. Stevens, *The Varieties of Human Temperament* (New York: Harper & Brothers, 1942), 298.

26 With a somatotype of 172. As Hersey points out, "that Batman as late as 1970 was still a Sheldonian mesomorph is proof that Sheldon's insight was still alive," *The Evolution of Allure*, 99.

assistant Barbara Honeyman Heath with the collaboration of physical education departments eager to improve female posture, health, and athleticism,
but they remained filed away and forgotten in the back rooms of college gym-
nasia. There they stayed until Honeyman Heath parted ways with Sheldon.
Denouncing his methods as fraudulent and his somatotypes inaccurate, she
contributed to the ruination of his career while advancing her own and joining
up with Margaret Mead to somatotype natives in Papua New Guinea.[27] Many
years later, Naomi Wolf, in her best-selling book *The Beauty Myth*, bitterly attacked men's appropriation of women's bodies through the collection of these
nude college fresh(wo)man photographs. As a young graduate of Vassar, she
remembered being party to the jokes of Dick Cavett, who had been invited
to speak at her graduate ceremony. His story was that a cache of posture (somatotype) photos taken of Vassar girls had been stolen, later to appear for sale
in New Haven's pornography black market. Cavett's punchline, aimed at the
traditional view of a female academic as all mind and no body, was that "the
photos found no buyers."[28]

Sustaining the Beauty Myth: The Female Body as Object of Health and Desire
Cavett's insinuation that men are more interested in a female's beauty than
her brains infuriated Wolf, who lamented that, despite feminist advances, and
the more legal and material hindrances that women have broken through, the
more strictly and heavily and cruelly images of female beauty have come to
weigh upon us. More women have more money and power than we have ever
had before, but in terms of how we feel about ourselves physically, we may actually be worse off than our un-liberated grandmothers.

Wolf attributed to the rise of photography an important historical role in dis-
seminating models of idealized femininity and beauty where the female body
was expected to look dramatically different from that of the man. Photography was invented in 1839 and, as Susan Sontag articulates so clearly, it inau-
gurated a new visual code, a body archive, where photographs could alter and

---

27 Patricia Vertinsky, "'Physique as Destiny': William H. Sheldon, Barbara Honeyman
    Heath and the Struggle for Hegemony in the Science of Somatotyping," *Canadian
    Bulletin of Medical History/Bulletin canadien d'histoire de la medicine* 24, no. 2 (2007):
    291–316.

28 Naomi Wolf, *The Beauty Myth* (Toronto: Vintage Books, 1990), 213; George L. Hersey,
    letter to the editor. "A Secret Lies Hidden in Vassar and Yale Nude Posture Photos," *New
    York Times*, July 3, 1992.

enlarge notions of what was worth looking at and what people had a right to observe.[29] North American society had begun to reflect the anxieties of middle-class Americans in discovering their bodies by placing a whole new emphasis upon the human form, but the notions that emerged about the ideal female form were in some respects more conservative than liberating. According to the dictates of science and philosophy that placed men in the public domain and contained women in the home, modern men and women were expected to look dramatically different from one another. If men and women were to occupy distinct roles, they had to look their parts, hence appearances were expected to testify to the maintenance of a social order based on visible distinctions.

Female beauty played a key element in defining women's existence during the Victorian era, acknowledging Ralph Waldo Emerson's dictum that beauty reaches its perfection in the human form and its height in women. Yet the pursuit of beauty was both class-based and double-edged, for it carried with it a promise of well-being and moral goodness, while also tempting women of means to become prey to the forces of narcissism and consumerism. While it was agreed that it was a woman's business to be beautiful and that "to be pretty was the natural desire of a girlish heart," feminists and health reformers decried those who endangered their health by slavishly following fashion, wearing tight corsets and narrow shoes, staying indoors, and avoiding exercise.

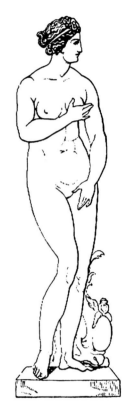

Line drawing of the Medici Venus.

In light of this dictum, social historians of women's fashion and beauty ideals have struggled to show how complex, contradictory, and controlling was much of the advice given to Victorian women about how to be beautiful and how to achieve a perfect body shape. The corset was a perfect example of the push and pull around fashion and beauty, as it was both an ever-present monitor and a sexualizing device, at once supportive yet restricting.[30] Aligned with this focus upon shape and appropriate size were successive endeavors to promote health through physical exercise, better eating habits, rational dress, and controlled sexuality. Lois Banner, for example, has characterized three successive types of ideal female forms which seemed to predominate among middle- and upper-class women of the nineteenth century, although these ideals of female beauty were differences in degree only and all models continued to vie for attention. Her broad characterizations of desirable female body architecture—the slender

29   Susan Sontag, *On Photography* (New York: Farrar, Straus and Giroux, 1978), 3.

30   Valerie Steele, *The Corset: A Cultural History* (New Haven, CT: Yale University Press, 2003).

"steel engraving" woman of the early Victorian period (Dickens' Little Dorritt, Eliot's Dorothea Brooke, and Brontë's Jane Eyre were all defined by their slight, pale bodies), followed by the plump and voluptuous woman of the second half of the century, which gave way to the more slender, athletic type at century's end—have served as a useful backdrop for scrutinizing calls for health reform alongside developing medical arguments that tended to limit female functions and mobility.[31]

Steel engraving, circa 1840.

Physicians initially argued that women were naturally small and frail until competition with health quackery pressed them to join forces with moral physiologists to support physical education and other health reforms which might fortify the female frame. Through hygienic conditioning, bathing and going to the seaside, chewing one's food properly, wearing electro-magnetic belts, or purging with laxatives and emetics, it was generally agreed that stronger, healthier, more muscular women could become better mothers and more attractive wives. Indeed, a number of purposive exercise training programs were developed for women during and after the antebellum years that competed with what Barbara Welter has called the "Cult of True Womanhood" and its view of submissive maidens.[32] Jan Todd has written extensively about these programs and their goal to mold 'real women' with strength, muscles, and vitality. These early exercise programs, she notes, which were often initially imported from Europe, particularly Great Britain, encouraged some women to have a new relationship to their bodies, to view them as trainable and more importantly controllable. In some cases, their desire to be strong women turned out to be the pathway to doing something important with their lives.[33] In her influential *Letters to the People on Health and Happiness*, female health reformer Catharine Beecher included "a line drawing of the Venus de Medici which, like most Greek representations of the feminine form, is full-bodied, natural-waisted and visibly athletic."[34] It was an image of a much larger, more physically fit woman than the wasp-waisted "steel engraving" woman seen in the popular magazine *Godey's Lady's Book* who, for Beecher, represented a means for women to be-

31   See Lois Banner, *American Beauty.* (New York: Alfred Knopf, 1983).

32   Barbara Welter, "The Cult of True Womanhood: 1820–1860," *American Quarterly* 18, no. 2 (1966).

33   Jan Todd, *Physical Culture and the Body Beautiful* (Macon, GA: Mercer University Press, 1998), 7.

34   Ibid., 161.

come stronger and more efficient—albeit in their assigned domestic role.[35]

At the same time, the effect of health reforms, increased education, and the growing number of non-working middle-class women in the postbellum years exacerbated male anxieties in an industrializing society increasingly fearful of a disintegrating social order. Some argue that this vogue among medical men for supporting the ideal of plump and voluptuous women was an effort to regain control of females by devaluing their minds and re-emphasizing their bodies. Large bosoms and swelling hips were extolled as a visual manifestation of woman's only purposeful role—maternity—deliberately restricting her opportunity for intellectual and physical pursuits. This, at any rate, was what Charlotte Perkins Gilman charged in her short story, "The Yellow Wallpaper," her bitter indictment of Dr Weir Mitchell's Rest Cure for neurasthenic women with its prescriptions of enforced bed rest and a plentiful diet of milk.[36] In her critique of Lois Banner's *American Beauty*, Sarah Stage provides a different argument: that the triumph of the voluptuous woman after mid-century marked to a certain extent "a triumph of the masses over the classes" given that a growing number of working-class girls, taking their cue from actresses and chorus girls, had begun to formulate their own ideals of beauty which often usurped the prevailing mode. The corset, she notes, remained in many respects a central feature in the costume of both the thin and the plump—and it could be associated with images of explosive fecundity and sexual energy as well as peep-show-style prurience. The voluptuous woman was simply a more vulgar exaggeration of the "steel engraving" lady.[37] In reality, both forms of female beauty were ultimately unsustainable as it became increasingly clear that healthy babies required fit mothers, and that fit mothers needed fresh air, exercise, and more space to breathe.

Popular standards of female beauty thus came to reflect the "cult of Hygeia" with its growing consensus around female health and exercise needs as the twentieth century dawned. Neither female frailty nor fleshy plumpness continued to be extolled as functional or as standards to emulate as the triumph

---

35   Kathryn Kish Sklar, *Catharine Beecher: A Study in American Domesticity* (New York: W.W. Norton, 1973).

36   Patricia Vertinsky, "A Militant Madonna: Charlotte Perkins Gilman, Feminism and Physical Culture," in *Freeing the Female Body: Inspirational Icons*, ed. F. Hong and J.A. Mangan (London: Frank Cass Publications, 2001).

37   Sarah Stage, "Seeing Through American Beauty," review of *American Beauty* by Lois W. Banner, *American Quarterly* 36, no. 2 (1984), 299.

Lillian Russell.

of the exercise movement, accelerated by the popularity of the bicycle, made it clear that no woman could be beautiful without exercise.[38] Renowned beauty and actress Lillian Russell, whose voluptuous hourglass figure had been applauded by fashion mavens on both sides of the Atlantic, tightened up her corset, went on a diet, and began working out with barbells as the Gibson Girl, tall, leggy, and slightly athletic, became the model to emulate. Russell, said the *New York Journal* unkindly, had over-indulged on fifteen-course meals and never moved much, and now the static pleasures of solid milky flesh were "moving out of fashion." The new ideal was incarnated by fellow actress Lillie Langtry, "the Jersey Lily," whose reputation as England's most beautiful woman was heightened by her liaison with the Prince of Wales; Langtry's Greek profile, wide shoulders, and passion for diet and exercise were perfectly suited to couturier Charles Worth's exquisite gowns. By 1920, the new aesthetic of a slim and increasingly young female beauty had been solidly established and recorded by the camera. Even before pictures began to move, fashion was emphasizing freer gestures and posture. The flapper, portrayed in constant motion, signified not simply a new ideal type, but a new public eye adjusted to the camera's vision.

These changing ideals of female beauty also reflected shifting attitudes toward sexual expression and eroticism. Victorian prudery had by now been challenged on many fronts, especially among the working classes and on the stage in the form of the muscular strong woman, the curvaceous chorus girl, and the exotic circus performer.[39]

Female Sex and Muscle on the Stage
In France, England, and the United States, the circuses vied with the music hall and cabaret as popular entertainments; all were fascinating examples of the potentially transgressive quality of popular entertainment forms as well as the strategies by which they were contained and their threats to middle-class respectability defused. Strongmen and strongwomen were particularly popular in the circus, where they would lift, push, or bend seemingly unbreakable and unbendable objects. "Catherine the Great" had motor cars driven across her body; she also caught a cannonball on the back of her neck. Katie Brumbach

---

38   Patricia Vertinsky, "Weighs and Means: Examining the Surveillance of Fat Bodies through Physical Education Practices in North America in the late 19th and early 20th Centuries," *Journal of Sport History* 35, no. 3 (2008): 402–20.

39   Steele, *The Corset: A Cultural History.*

from Vienna, the main attraction of the Ringling Brothers Circus, was billed as the world's strongest and most beautiful woman. At over six feet tall, with bulging seventeen-inch biceps and twenty-six-inch thighs, she was able to lift her 165-pound husband above her head with one hand and carry a 600-pound cannon on her shoulder. After supposedly beating strongman Eugen Sandow in a weightlifting context in New York, she adopted the stage name Sandwina. German (or perhaps New Jersey)-born Minerva, was one of the most successful strongwomen of all time. Performing in circuses and on the vaudeville stage, she could lift 700 pounds from the floor with two hands, break horseshoes, and catch twenty-pound cannonballs.[40] When she lifted eighteen men at a popular resort near Washington, DC, in 1895, she was described in the *Washington Post* as "a marvelous specimen of muscle."[41] This reversal of gender roles was, of course, a common trope on the vaudeville stage where the novelty lay in a woman doing the "muscular" work usually performed by the man—the trick lay in making her mastery of male feats a surprising element in an otherwise feminine performance and persona.[42] Around the same time that Minerva was raising great weights, strongwoman Charmion from Sacramento, California, was raising eyebrows with her unusual strength-related acts and her risqué striptease performances on the trapeze. Impressive and provocative, her stunts and eroticism generated a devoted, and mostly male, fan base, including Thomas Edison, who enthusiastically filmed her "Trapeze Disrobing Act" in 1901.[43]

When Florenz Ziegfeld, Jr. presented one-time circus performer and internationally known strongman Eugen Sandow at the Chicago World's Fair in 1893, women were invited backstage to titter at the sight and feel of his muscles (albeit in the guise of donating to a charitable cause).[44] It was recognition that

Artist John Held Jr. created this sports-mad flapper in 1925.

---

40 Jan Todd, "The Mystery of Minerva," *Iron Game History* 1, no. 2 (1990). In a second article, Todd points out that it is more likely that Minerva was born in New Jersey, not Germany. Jan Todd, "Sex, Murder, Suicide. New Revelations about the Mystery of Minerva," *Iron Game History* 10, no. 4 (Jan 2009).

41 "Wednesday and the Fourth at Riverview," *Washington Post*, July 3, 1895.

42 M. Alison Kibler, *Ladies of Rank: Gender and Cultural Hierarchy in American Vaudeville*. Chapel Hill and London: University of North Carolina Press, 1999, 146.

43 Thomas Edison, "Trapeze Disrobing Act," Stock Footage Collection, http://www.archive.org/details/SF120. See also Peta Tait, *Circus Bodies: Cultural Identity in Aerial Performance* (New York: Routledge, 2005) and Helen Stoddart, *Rings of Desire, Circus History and Representation* (Manchester, UK: Manchester University Press, 2000).

44 Charles Higham, *Ziegfeld* (Chicago: Regnery, 1972), 10–12.

Eugen Sandow.

the display of the male muscular body as a sexualized object was turning it from a site of production to a site for consumption—a traditional feminine position.[45] Sandow (the "father of modern bodybulding") was quite aware of the erotic response he could evoke from his posing, and though he sometimes insisted upon ladies-only posing sessions, photographs and cigarette cards of neoclassical "erect" poses in which he appeared clad in a false fig leaf were widely circulated in the homosexual community at the turn of the century. This shifting of the sexual terrain encouraged strongwomen as well as strongmen to take possession of their bodies in a new way and display them on the stage, even while fitness educators and doctors railed at the physical and moral dangers of an exaggerated muscular system. Leading American physical educator and doctor, Dudley Allen Sargent, complained that "piles of parasitic muscles required an undue amount of nourishment lowering bodily efficiency and making athletes into physiological profligates."[46] These contradictory viewpoints in the physical culture movement of the late nineteenth and early twentieth centuries functioned in some respects as "ideological release points," paradoxically enabling establishment doctors to retain their authority while at the same time allowing subcultures to develop and challenge their views.[47]

Sandow's rival, Bernarr Macfadden, relished the enormous potential of physical culture commerce where the body could become "a design space wherein the principles of surveillance, discipline and efficiency might be employed by anyone who could afford a postcard or a magazine."[48] As the flamboyant and self-proclaimed "father of physical culture," he grafted an enormously successful publishing career onto his earlier success as a strength performer. Unlike Sandow, who was rumored to enjoy the company of young men as well as women, Macfadden was particularly interested in sex and the well-built female body, especially the female bust; well-formed breasts were evidence of muscular health, sexual attractiveness, and reproductive fitness. He married four times and was preoccupied with being strong enough to produce a new genera-

45   Andrew Perchuk and Helaine Posner, eds. *The Masculine Masquerade. Masculinity and Representation* (Cambridge, MA: MIT Press, 1995).

46   Dudley Allen Sargent, "The Dangers of Athletic Training," *American Medicine*, 13 (1907): 500.

47   Patricia Vertinsky, "Making and Marking Gender: Bodybuilding and the Medicalization of the Body from One Century's End to Another," *Sport in Society* 2, no. 1 (1999).

48   Michael Anton Budd, *The Sculpture Machine: Physical Culture and Body Politics in the Age of Empire* (New York: New York University Press, 1997), 121.

tion of physical culture families. We must accept the biological fact that man is an animal, he insisted, and in order to be successful he must first be a fine, strong, wholesome, beautiful animal.[49] The medical profession complained that his *Physical Culture* magazines reeked of sex and a fixation upon muscle ... a fixation that carries along with it narcissism and suspect sexual preferences."[50] His arrest by anti-pornography crusader Anthony Comstock in 1905 was not just anxiety over the mass circulation of nearly nude photographs, but also that he was exhibiting "athletic girls" at a Madison Square Garden exhibition. In fact, Macfadden's perfect woman contest displayed women who had similar physical proportions as those the respectable Dudley Allen Sargent exhibited and appreciated as composites of a typical American female student, at the World's Fair (who, in turn, were also modeled along the pure lines of classical Greek statues of beautiful women). These statues, said Sargent, illustrated the highest ideals of feminine beauty and loveliness in figure. In fact, both the ideal woman contest—won by Emma Newkirk from Santa Monica, California—and the ideal student composites were developed to show that all beauty had its roots in a physically active lifestyle. But, as Macfadden added pointedly, "there can be no beauty without muscles."[51] He continued to publish *Physical Culture* for decades, and by 1955, sales reached over a million copies a year.[52]

Physical Fitness and the New Woman: How to Get Strong and How to Stay So
Martha Verbrugge has described how the new model of able-bodied womanhood emerged in the early years of the twentieth century. Compared to her weak consumptive sister of the 1800s, this "new woman" had a robust figure, wore sensible clothes, exercised outdoors, and exuded health.[53] However, the dilemma of where health and femininity should meet remained contentious in many areas of society and on both sides of the Atlantic.

---

49   See James Whorton, *Crusaders for Fitness, The History of American Health Reformers* (Princeton, NJ: Princeton University Press, 1982), 296–301.

50   Vertinsky, "Making and Marking Gender," 11.

51   Jan Todd, "Bernarr Macfadden. Reformer of the Feminine Form," in *Sport and Exercise Science: Essays in the History of Sport Medicine*, ed. Jack Berryman and Roberta J. Park (Urbana and Chicago: University of Illinois Press, 1992), 226–27.

52   Tim Benzie, "Judy Garland at the Gym—Gay Magazines and Gay Bodybuilding," *Continuum: Journal of Media and Cultural Studies*, 14, no. 2 (2000).

53   Martha Verbrugge, *Able-Bodied Womanhood: Personal Health and Social Change in Nineteenth Century Boston* (New York: Oxford University Press, 1988), 196.

Feminist author Charlotte Perkins Gilman was one of a swelling group of first-wave feminists demanding that women be allowed to control their own bodies and extend the parameters of their physical capabilities. When she wrote her novel *Herland* in 1915, it was a paean to her dedication to female physical fitness gleaned from William Blaikie's highly popular manual, *How to Get Strong and How to Stay So*.[54] Blaikie had called upon women and girls to develop idle muscles in pursuit of vigorous health, and use vigorous exercise to develop chests, backs, and arms, in order to grow from a strong and healthy child to a hearty vigorous woman. Gilman had more radical suggestions, however, including a total redefinition of male and female roles. In *Herland*, there were no men at all; they had all been killed off, allowing a female community to flourish through a kind of virgin birth which only yielded girl children. In this Utopia, Gilman's ideal women built spacious parks and gardens to encourage athletic development and tilled collective fields to produce nutritious food. They were agile, strong, and healthy in body and mind, and their organizational form allowed them a life of comparative freedom and great activity that Gilman yearned for but never achieved.[55]

Herland, of course, echoed the ancient Greek myth of the Amazons, a strong and fearless female tribe governed by queen Hippolyta where the women were said to have cut off one breast in order to shoot arrows and fight like men. The myth of the Amazon is one of female power, strength, and agency, and as Martha Banta has shown in *Imaging American Women*, it traditionally served as a wondrously ample convention for displaying the warrior spirit needed for progress in the modern world: the protecting mother angel, the intrepid Red Cross nurse, the plunge toward burlesque, the suffragist, and the "new woman."[56] The Amazon myth is also the only classical myth that speaks of a matriarchal culture that excludes men altogether, hence it played a formative role within an emerging lesbian 'new woman' culture in the early twentieth century.

Artists such as Romaine Brooks (an American living in Europe) produced powerful images of feminine vitality and power at a particularly volatile time

---

54   William Blaikie, *How to Get Strong and How to Stay So* (New York: Harper & Brothers, 1884).

55   Charlotte Perkins Gilman, *Herland* (1915. New York: Dover, 1998). See also Li-Wen Chang, "Economics, Evolution and Feminism in Charlotte Perkins Gilman's Utopian Fiction," *Women's Studies* 39, no. 4 (2009): 319–348.

56   Martha Banta, *Imaging American Women: Idea and Ideals in Cultural History* (New York: Columbia University Press, 1897), 465–99.

within European culture, revealing the growing tensions between traditional inscriptions of masculinity and femininity. Her series of paintings of "heroic femininity" was followed by a group of "Amazons in the drawing room," which showed a transition in the search for an idealistic representation of the female figure to bold images of independent women, most of whom were sexually and/ or socially connected to her lesbian circle. They represented a self-conscious attempt to produce and circulate a new image of twentieth-century woman— the lesbian—an image of powerful androgynous femininity, the cross-dressing warrior woman whose hard athletic body and aggressive confrontational stance radically destabilized the gendered categories of male and female.[57]

Babe Didrikson.

The issue of sexuality loomed particularly large where the female sporting body was concerned, for despite the emergence of the modern athletic woman during the interwar years—those decades that have been called the golden age of sport—most people could not separate the concept of athletic superiority from its cultural affiliation with masculine sport and the male, muscular body. Dudley Allen Sargent still wondered whether female athleticism would turn women into masculine facsimiles of the opposite sex. And when Babe Didrikson burst onto the scene in the 1930s with her superb athletic accomplishments, journalists pointed relentlessly to her "mannish" appearance. The athletic virtuosity and "piano-wire muscles" of "the Babe" did not represent the controlled and efficient womanliness that middle-class maternal physical educators promoted; nor did she look like pretty Canadian Olympic figure skating sensation Barbara Ann Scott. Instead, pointing to her "masculine" appearance, journalists labeled her a "Muscle Moll" while describing English Channel swimmer Gertrude Ederle as a strapping girl with muscles of steel. Susan Cahn's detailed analysis of gender, sexuality, and sport during these years shows how observers puzzled over reconciling their belief in the masculinity of sport with the unsettling fact of female athletic accomplishment. Was it possible that the Amazonian athlete might be not only unattractive but unattracted to men? Indeed, might she prefer women? In *Technics and Civilization,* Lewis Mumford exemplified the male sports hero as virile and courageous. "If the hero is a girl," he reasoned, "her qualities must be Amazonian in nature. The sports hero represents the masculine virtues, the Mars complex, as the popular motion picture actress or the bathing beauty

57   Whitney Chadwick, *Amazons in the Drawing Room: The Art of Romaine Brooks* (Berkeley: University of California Press, 2000).

contest represents Venus."[58] How then to resolve the incongruity of a female Mars? Media commentators found the answer in persuading the Amazonian female athlete to shed the character of Mars and become Venus.[59]

"The Babe" resolved the threat of seeming masculine by withdrawing from track and field, getting married, feminizing her appearance, and returning in the late 1940s, suitably clothed, as an unbeatable champion golfer. Nevertheless, the exposure of working muscles continued to provoke hostile claims that muscularity caused a masculinization of the female body and detracted from essential femaleness. It remains a recurring phenomenon to this day despite the massive advances in women's sport as a result of Title IX, the section of the US Educational Amendment Act that in 1972 mandated equal funding for girls' sports.

The Conundrum of Somatic Femininity: Barbie vs. Pudgy Stockton
As is so often the case after a crisis, the years following both world wars provoked a deepening concern about health, national fitness, and the shape of the nation—as well as the shape and mobility of the woman. World War I showed quite clearly that women could replace men in work that would never have been thought suitable before, and though their wartime jobs were removed from them at war's end, many had developed new ideas about their own strength, mobility, and independence. In the 1920s, Coco Chanel was called "the inventor of twentieth-century woman" by creating fashions for the simple boyish look of the flapper, cutting loose from traditional constraints by flattening their bosoms and lowering their waists.

During World War II, women were again called upon to dedicate their health and strength to the war effort, and American anthropometrists, continuing their quest to elaborate a scientifically sanctioned notion of a normative female body, sought to show how she was a definite improvement over her grandmother of the 1890s (the composite female body that had been displayed by Dudley Allen Sargent at the World's Fair in 1893). In 1945, Robert Latou Dickinson and Abram Belskie introduced one of the most celebrated and widely publicized anthropometric models of the century, Norm and Norma, the average American male and female. Described in the press as an ideal young

---

58 Lewis Mumford, *Technics and Civilization* (1st edition, 1933; New York: Harbinger Books, 1963), quoted in John Hoberman, *Sport and Political Ideology* (Austin: University of Texas Press, 1984), 89.

59 Susan Cahn, *Coming On Strong: Gender and Sexuality in Twentieth-Century Women's Sports* (New York: Maxwell Macmillan, 1994), 213.

woman, "Norma was said to be everything an American woman should be in time of war: she was fit, strong bodied and at the peak of her reproductive potential."[60] It was an image ripe for the conservative decades following the turmoil of war in which Rosie the Riveter returned from the factory to her rightful role as wife, mother, and homemaker. But it was challenged almost immediately by images of fashion models and movie stars introduced by the entertainment industry and a burgeoning consumer culture. In 1947, Christian Dior's "New Look" turned the fashion world upside down by launching a new feminine shape with a tiny corseted waist, full bosom and hips, and bouffant petticoated skirts. Outraged feminists complained to the press, but the ladylike and glamorous figure launched by Dior dominated the 1950s.[61]

Dior's New Look also presaged the 1959 debut of Mattel's Barbie, the teenage fashion doll that rose quickly to become the top-selling toy in the United States. Now fifty years old, the Barbie doll remains Mattel's most popular toy, with one sold every two seconds worldwide. Mattel's marketers have worked hard to keep Barbie relevant to changes in popular culture over the years, but what is striking is that her hyper-slender body and torpedo-like breasts have remained fundamentally unchanged over the years. Her hair, skin tone, and facial features have all changed, but her measurements and proportions have not altered significantly over her fifty years of existence. What makes Barbie such a perfect icon of late capitalist constructions of femininity, conclude Jacqueline Urla and Alan Swedlund, "is the way in which her persona pairs endless consumption with the achievement of femininity and the appearance of an appropriately gendered body."[62] It supports a beauty myth fueled by the fashion, cosmetic, and weight-loss industries, and diverts the attention of girls and women from aspiring to develop and show off a strong and muscular body.

Not all girls and women, however, for as the illustrations in this book demonstrate so vividly, there have always been women who preferred to build their bodies and show their strength, whether or not they also tried to fit acceptable feminine stereotypes. At the same time that Barbie was being introduced to

---

60   Jacqueline Urla and Alan C. Swedlund, "The Anthropometry of Barbie: Unsettling Ideas of the Feminine Body in Popular Culture," In *Deviant Bodies. Critical Perspectives on Difference in Science and Popular Culture*, ed. Jennifer Terry and Jacqueline Urla (Bloomington and Indianapolis: Indiana University Press, 1995), 290.

61   Angela Holdsworth, *Out of the Doll's House: The Story of Women in the Twentieth Century* (London: BBC Books, 1988).

62   Urla and Swedlund, "The Anthropometry of Barbie," 281.

teenagers during the Cold War years, Pudgy Stockton was exuding a graceful and energetic femininity at Muscle Beach in California while becoming a pioneer in women's bodybuilding and weightlifting. In 1948, she was selected "Miss Physical Culture Venus" by Bernarr Macfadden for her unusual combination of strength, athletic ability, and shapeliness, and over a decade later she appeared on the cover of *Muscular Development* as the "Queen of Muscledom." Her popularity in the media, through professional appearances and magazine articles, persuaded more and more women to begin to see that muscles could be feminine, strength an asset, and working out fun. "Pudgy Stockton was something brand new," wrote Elizabeth McCracken in her *New York Times* article, "The Belle of the Barbell." "Every inch and ounce of her body refuted the common wisdom that training with weights turned women manly and musclebound. She was splendid as a work of art but undoubtedly, thrillingly, flesh, blood, breath."[63]

Reflecting on the extraordinary influence of Pudgy Stockton on strongwomen such as herself and Lisa Lyon, the first "modern" woman bodybuilder, Jan Todd showed how femininity was toughening up.[64] She presaged the hope that the show of female muscles was becoming a normal part of girls' and women's everyday lives—a body for herself—for her own use. Talking about her own pursuit to be a strong woman, Leslie Heywood wonders whether the image of the strong muscular female will help women in general become strong: "Precarious though my faith may be, I have to believe that it does. I have to believe that consciously or unconsciously, intentionally or no, any babe who sports a muscle symbolically strikes a blow against traditional ideas about male supremacy ... I have to believe that any woman with muscles makes a statement in support of women's equality, self-realization, women's rights. A woman with muscles shouts out about female sovereignty, about women's right to be for themselves not others, about their right to exist, take up space."[65]

---

63 Elizabeth McCracken, "The Belle of the Barbell," *New York Times*, 2006, http://www.nytimes.com/2006/12/31/magazine/31stockton.t.html.

64 Jan Todd, "The Legacy of Pudgy Stockton," *Iron Game History* 2, no. 1 (1992), 5–7.

65 Leslie Heywood, *Bodymakers: A Cultural Anatomy of Women's Body Building* (New Brunswick, NJ: Rutgers University Press, 1998), 191.

Ginnastica femminile

Bibliography

Banner, Lois W. *American Beauty*. New York: Alfred Knopf, 1983.

Banta, Martha. *Imaging American Women: Idea and Ideals in Cultural History*. New York: Columbia University Press, 1987.

Bartky, Sandra Lee. "Foucault, Femininity, and the Modernization of Patriarchal Power." In *Feminism and Foucault: Reflections on Resistance*, edited by I. Diamond and L. Quinby. Boston, MA: Northeastern University Press, 1988.

Benzie, Tim. "Judy Garland at the Gym—Gay Magazines and Gay Bodybuilding." *Continuum: Journal of Media and Cultural Studies* 14, no. 2 (2000): 159–70.

Berger, John. *Ways of Seeing*: Based on the BBC Television Series. London: Penguin Group, 1972.

Blaikie, William. *How to Get Strong and How to Stay So*. New York: Harper and Brothers, 1884.

Bordo, Susan. "Reading the Slender Body." In *Body/Politics: Women and the Discourses of Science*, edited by M. Jacobus, E. Fox Keller, and S. Shuttleworth. New York: Routledge, 1990.

Boyle, Ellexis. "The Intertextual Terminator: The Role of Film in Branding 'Arnold Schwarzenegger.'" *Journal of Communication Inquiry* 34, no.1 (2010): 42–60.

Budd, Michael Anton. *The Sculpture Machine: Physical Culture and Body Politics in the Age of Empire*. New York: New York University Press, 1997.

Chadwick, Whitney. *Amazons in the Drawing Room: The Art of Romaine Brooks*. Berkeley: University of California Press; Washington, DC: National Museum of Women in the Arts, 2000.

Dobbins, Bill. "Female Muscle: What's It About; How I Photograph It." Bill Dobbins Female Physique Art Gallery. http://www.billdobbins.net/PUBLIC/pages/femuscle.htm.

Cahn, Susan. *Coming On Strong: Gender and Sexuality in Twentieth Century Women's Sport*. New York: Free Press; Toronto: Maxwell Macmillan, 1994.

Chang, Li-Wen. "Economics, Evolution and Feminism in Charlotte Perkins Gilman's Utopian Fiction." *Women's Studies* 39, no. 4 (2010): 319–48.

Connell, R.W. *Masculinities*. NSW, Australia: Allen & Unwin, 2005.

Davis, Lorraine Anne. "Investing in Photography." In *Cultures of Economy—Economics of Culture*, edited by Jackson Lears and Jens Van Scherpenberg, 167–202. Heidelberg: Universitätsverlag, Winter, 2004.

Dutton, Kenneth R. *The Perfectible Body: The Western Ideal of Male Physical Development*. New York: Continuum, 1995.

Dyer, Richard. "The White Man's Muscles." In *The Masculinity Studies Reader*, edited by R. Adams and D. Savran. Oxford: Blackwell Publishers, 2002.

Edison, Thomas. "Trapeze Disrobing Act." Stock Footage Collection, 1901. Standard 4:3. http://www.archive.org/details/SF120.

Ehrenreich, Barbara, and Barbara Maddux. "The Real Truth About the Female Body." *Time*, March 8, 1999. http://www.time.com/time/magazine/article/0,9171,990379-1,00.html.

Ewing, William A. *The Body: Photographs of the Human Form*. San Francisco: Chronicle Books, 2004.

Fowler, Orson Squire. *Phrenology and Physiology Explained and Applied to Education, and Self Improvement: Including the Intellectual and Moral Education and Government of Children*. New York: O.S. and L.N. Fowler, 1843.

————. *Private Lectures on Perfect Men, Women and Children, in Happy Families*. New York: E.W. Fowler, 1880.

Gilman, Charlotte Perkins. *Herland*. 1915. New York: Dover, 1998.

Hersey, George L. *The Evolution of Allure: Sexual Selection from the Medici Venus to the Incredible Hulk*. Cambridge, MA: MIT Press, 1996.

————. "A Secret Lies Hidden in Vassar and Yale Nude Posture Photos." Letter to the Editor. *New York Times*, July 3, 1992.

Heywood, Leslie. *Bodymakers: A Cultural Anatomy of Women's Body Building*. New Brunswick, NJ: Rutgers University Press, 1998.

Higham, Charles. *Ziegfeld*. Chicago: Regnery, 1972.

Hoberman, John. *Sport and Political Ideology*. Austin: University of Texas Press, 1984.

Holdsworth, Angela. *Out of the Doll's House: The Story of Women in the Twentieth Century*. London: BBC Books, 1988.

Holmlund, Christine Anne. "Visible Differences and Flex Appeal: The Body, Sex, Sexuality, and Race in the Pumping Iron Films." In *Out of Bounds: Sport, Media and the Politics of Identity*, edited by A. Baker and T. Boyd. Bloomington and Indianapolis: Indiana University Press, 1997.

Kibler, M. Alison. *Ladies of Rank: Gender and Cultural Hierarchy in American Vaudeville*. Chapel Hill and London: The University of North Carolina Press, 1999.

Klein, Alan M. "Pumping Iron." *Society* 22, no.6 (1985): 68–75.

Kuriyama, Shigehisa. *The Expressiveness of the Body and the Divergence of Greek and Chinese Medicine*. New York: Zone Books, 1999.

Levin, Dan. "Here She Is, Miss, Well, What?" *Sports Illustrated*, March 17, 1980.

Magill, D. "Spectacular Male Bodies and Jazz Age Celebrity Culture." In *Framing Celebrity: New Directions in Celebrity Culture*, edited by S. Holmes and S. Redmond. London and New York: Routledge, 2006.

Mansfield, Alan, and Barbara McGinn. "Pumping Irony: The Muscular and the Feminine." In *Body Matters: Essays on the Sociology of the Body*, edited by S. Scott, and D. Morgan. London: Falmer, 1993.

McCracken, Elizabeth. "The Belle of the Barbell." *New York Times*, December 31, 2006. http://www.nytimes.com/20006/12/31/magazine/31stockton.t.html.

Mumford, Lewis. *Technics and Civilization*. 1933. New York: Harbinger Books, 1963.

Perchuk, Andrew, and Helaine Posner, eds. *The Masculine Masquerade: Masculinity and Representation*. Cambridge, MA: MIT Press, 1995.

Sargent, Dudley Allen. "The Dangers of Athletic Training." *American Medicine* 13 (1907): 500.

Schwarzenegger, Arnold. *Arnold: The Education of a Bodybuilder*. New York: Simon and Schuster, 1977.

Sheldon, William H., with S.S. Stevens. *The Varieties of Temperament: A Psychology of Constitutional Differences*. New York: Harper & Brothers, 1942.

Sklar, Kathryn Kish. *Catharine Beecher: A Study in American Domesticity*. New York: W.W. Norton, 1973.

Sontag, Susan. *On Photography*. New York: Farrar, Straus and Giroux, 1978.

Stage, Sarah. "Review: Seeing Through American Beauty." *American Quarterly* 36, no. 2 (Summer 1984): 297–302.

Steele, Valerie. *The Corset: A Cultural History*. New Haven, CT: Yale University Press, 2003.

Stoddart, Helen. *Rings of Desire: Circus History and Representation*. Manchester, UK: Manchester University Press, 2000.

Tait, Peta. *Circus Bodies: Cultural Identity in Aerial Performance*. New York: Routledge, 2005.

The Washington Post. "Wednesday and the Fourth at Riverview." July 3, 1895.

Todd, Jan. *Physical Culture and the Body Beautiful*. Macon, GA: Mercer University Press, 1998.

———. "The Legacy of Pudgy Stockton." *Iron Game History* 2, no. 1 (Jan 1992): 5–7.

———. "The Mystery of Minerva." *Iron Game History* 1, no. 2 (1990): 14–21.

———. "Sex! Murder! Suicide! New Revelations about the 'Mystery of Minerva.'" *Iron Game History* 10, no. 4 (Jan 2009): 7–21.

———. "Bernarr Macfadden: Reformer of Feminine Form." In *Sport and Exercise Science: Essays in the History of Sport Medicine*, edited by Jack Berryman and

Roberta J. Park. Urbana and Chicago: University of Illinois Press, 1992.

Urla, Jacqueline, and Alan C. Swedlund. "The Anthropometry of Barbie: Unsettling Ideas of the Feminine Body in Popular Culture." In *Deviant Bodies: Critical Perspectives on Difference in Science and Popular Culture*, edited by Jennifer Terry and Jacqueline Urla. Bloomington and Indianapolis: Indiana University Press, 1995.

Verbrugge, Martha. *Able-Bodied Womanhood: Personal Health and Social Change in Nineteenth-Century Boston*. New York: Oxford University Press, 1988.

Vertinsky, Patricia. "A Militant Madonna: Charlotte Perkins Gilman, Feminism and Physical Culture." In *Freeing the Female Body: Inspirational Icons*, edited by F. Hong and J. A. Mangan. London: Frank Cass Publications, 2001.

———. "Embodying Normalcy: Anthropometry and the Long Arm of William Sheldon's Somatotyping Project." *Journal of Sport History* 29, no. 1 (2002): 95–133.

———. "Making and Marking Gender: Bodybuilding and the Medicalization of the Body from One Century's End to Another." *Sport in Society* 2, no. 1 (1999): 1–24.

———. "Physique as Destiny: William H. Sheldon, Barbara Honeyman Heath and the Struggle for Hegemony in the Science of Somatotyping." *Canadian Bulletin of Medical History/Bulletin canadien d'histoire de la medicine* 24, no. 2 (2007): 291–316.

———. "Weighs and Means: Examining the Surveillance of Fat Bodies through Physical Education Practices in the late 19th and early 20th Centuries." *Journal of Sport History* 35, no. 3 (2008): 402–20.

Welter, Barbara. "The Cult of True Womanhood: 1820–1860." *American Quarterly* 18, no. 2 (1966): 151–74.

Whorton, James. *Crusaders for Fitness: The History of American Health Reformers*. Princeton, NJ: Princeton University Press, 1982.

Wolf, Naomi. *The Beauty Myth*. Toronto: Vintage Books, 1990.

FOREMOTHERS

The most public and visible ways that muscular women could make a living in the nineteenth and twentieth centuries was as professional or theatrical strongwomen. On the vaudeville and music hall stages of the world, these performers would lift heavy weights, juggle cannonballs, support pianos, or hoist their male partners into the air with ridiculous ease. Audiences paid to see their feats of strength and endurance. Because they needed images, posters, and advertisements to promote themselves, professional strongwomen have left the largest and most easily accessible record of female muscularity and the earliest records of their lives in the limelight of history.

No matter how glamorous or attractive they might have seemed, most women found it difficult to live decent lives by the sweat of their powdered brows or the strength of their physiques. At the lowest end of the strongwoman career ladder were the street performers, who, often with their male counterparts, would typically spread a threadbare carpet on a street corner and lift weights or otherwise display their prowess in the hopes that passersby would toss a few coins in front of them.

Only slightly better off were the fair and carnival artists who set up temporary booths at the carnivals that liberally peppered the European year. These events operated for only a few weeks and then moved on to the next location. It was a hard life, but at least these performers could charge an admission fee and not rely solely on the charity of the crowd. Many strongmen and wrestlers operated this way, and their shows almost always featured at least one strongwoman or lady wrestler to liven up the performances.

At the highest end of the scale were the variety theater or circus artists whose shows included elaborate acts, daring feats, and brilliant costumes. Beautiful posters announced their performances, often in places of honor on the program. Strongmen turns (i.e., acts) became quite popular in the heyday of vaudeville and music halls, and although they were much rarer, strongwomen occasionally showed up on the bill. A very few women achieved fame and modest fortune by virtue of their theatrical strength performances—many with stage names that conjured up a mythical or ferocious image: Athleta, Athelda, Jaguarina, Herculina, Vulcana, and others all trod the boards of the vaudeville stage or performed in the ring of an important circus.

Many of these professional strongwomen presented challenges to the men in the audience. They frequently dared any male in the theater to compare his strength to the woman's. Since these tests were carefully orchestrated and almost always involved either trickery or a specialized skill, the man usually came away defeated. The stunts varied with the performers, but most were similar to the exploits performed by their male counterparts and usually involved a certain amount of strength—and often a generous dollop of deception.

In the early images of strongwomen, there is almost always an impulse to balance the subject's strength with her femininity. Thus women will toss heavy weights about, but they pose demurely and gracefully, usually in lacy costumes. One or both of the models' hands are often held behind her back in a submissive stance, and they almost never flex their muscles in any significant way. The most that the viewer can expect is the crossed arms of a traditional strongman pose.

Interest in strength performers also profited from the physical culture and health craze that began in Europe and North America in the middle of the nineteenth century. After fitness and exercise writers began to point out the restorative benefits of regular physical exertion, many people worked out at home, in gymnasiums and schools. This new interest in various "exercise cures" brought muscular strength to the attention of middle-class men and women as never before. It now seemed possible to re-form and build new bodies from the untrained flesh of ordinary city dwellers, and this, in turn, focused attention on the muscularity of others who had trained their physiques to a state of near perfection. It was at this time that professional strongmen and strongwomen emerged from street corners and circus tents to create a new form of entertainment.

06. This engraving from around the turn of the nineteenth century is one of the earliest representations of a professional strongwoman that has survived. Although her name and nationality have been lost (though she is probably German), this illustration shows her performing an amazing feat. She holds three heavy ship's anchors (one in her teeth) in addition to four weights marked 225. Whether pounds or kilograms, either way the lift is impossible.

07. Among the earliest strongwomen whose names have come down to us is the subject of this lithograph: Elise Serafin Luftmann. Apparently from a German-speaking region of Bohemia, she performed all over central Europe. Luftmann was famous for her ability to lift heavy weights and to juggle cannonballs. This illustration dates c. 1830.

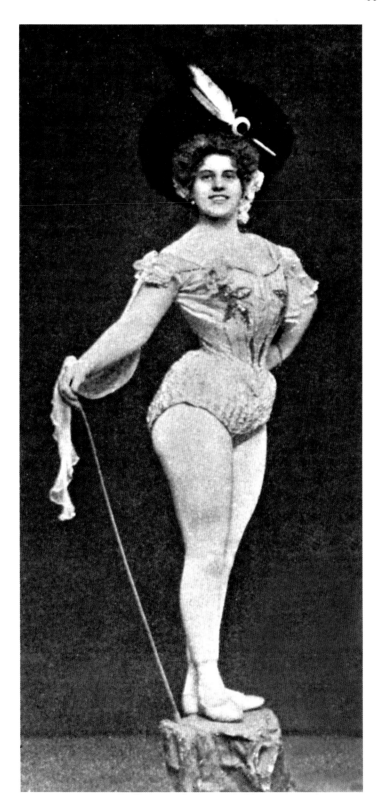

08. Annette Secchi was a renowned circus horsewoman. In her heyday her superb figure garnered even more praise than her horse-riding abilities. Here she displays the "hourglass" figure that was so prized in the late-nineteenth century. Female circus athletes were among the most common representatives of female muscularity, and their strenuous professions assured a tight and firm physique. Equestriennes were particularly popular because they combined elegance, balance, and skill with developed bodies and tight clothing.

09. All the great riders in the early years of the circus were Italians. Esterina Pissiuti, a member of a very famous family of equestrians from Italy, did complicated flips and gymnastic routines on the backs of galloping horses. Esterina's muscular thighs show the effect of many hours balancing on a horse's hindquarters. Before the modern obsession with breasts, it was women's hips and legs that attracted the salacious attention of most men; many of these early photos pander to that interest.

10. A way to diffuse male worries about women being too strong and threatening was to portray them in photos that emphasized their grace and beauty rather than their mass and musculature. Trapeze artists like this one had highly developed arms and upper bodies; it is significant that the photographer chose not to emphasize those parts of the subject's anatomy. Although her name and date are unknown, this gymnast is almost certainly a circus or music hall performer from the 1890s.

11. Madame Doublier had a strongwoman act in late nineteenth-century France. She lifted weights and barbells, the most spectacular part being when she raised a heavy loaded cannon and shot it. All very spectacular, it was a complete fake. The cannon was made of hollow zinc and her weights were phony. Still, she certainly looked the part of a professional strongwoman.

12. This rare cabinet photo, c. 1885, is one of the earliest representations of a professional strongwoman in action. Unusually for the time, the anonymous strongwoman is not posed in a graceful, balletic posture; rather, she wears a studded leather skirt and lifts various heavy weights—an unrepentantly powerful athlete showing the world what she can do. The photographer was Wendt of Boonton, New Jersey.

13. The anonymous lady in these pictures was featured on the back page of *The New York Standard* from 1894, a publication for those euphemistically called "sporting gentlemen." The subject was credited as "the strongest woman in the world," and is shown flexing, posing, and reclining. The photo of her back and biceps is one of the few from this time that dared to show a female flexing her muscles in imitation of the most famous professional strongman of the time, Eugen Sandow (1867–1925).

THE STANDARD.

FEMININE STRENGTH IN REPOSE.

EASY.

A MERE NOTHING.

MUSCLES OF BACK AND ARM.

BICEPS A PUGILIST MIGHT ENVY.

AT REST.

TENSE.

AN IMITATION OF SANDOW'S FAMOUS POSE.
THE STRONGEST WOMAN IN THE WORLD.
Compare her with Sandow.

14. By 1896, when these charming illustrations appeared in the magazine *Penny Fiction*, female athletes had become common enough that the popular press could poke gentle fun at them. The lady in this series of drawings lifts, supports, tosses around, and generally proves herself stronger than her male companion. The title of the sketches, "Parlor Gymnastics," refers both to the physical tricks and to the symbolic power that women were thought to have over impressionable young gentlemen.

PARLOR GYMNASTICS.

15. This lithograph from 1897 titled "La Femme Hercule" (the Lady Hercules) shows a French strongwoman performing on the streets. She supports her male counterpart while lying on mangy carpets. The fascinating part comes in the reversal of roles, since the woman is the strong "understander" (the athlete who supports the one above) while the man is the prop or decoration. This scene depicts the lowest point on the performing scale: strongmen and women who set up their meager displays on the streets in order to get a bit of change from the throng around them. It was a precarious existence at best, and most who engaged in it ended up miserable and poor.

Flossie La Blanche

In Extraordinary Feats of Strength

Lifting heavy weights with an ease and grace marvelous to contemplate.

Breaking heavy chains and lifting twelve men.   Making one lift of 2000 pounds.

Musical Director   -   HARRY JONES

Closing with a Screaming Farce by Entire Company

COME ONE! COME ALL!!

Don't miss it.   Miss your breakfast, dinner and supper, but don't miss this show.   Doors open at 2 and 7.30.   Performances start at 2.30 and 8.15.

 LOCATED ON MAIN STREET

Entrance to Tent between Steady's Music Store and Savings Bank.

General Admission to All   =   10 Cents

ith Reserved Seat, 20c.   Box Seats, 25c

16. Flossie La Blanche was an American strongwoman who traveled throughout New England and eastern Canada in the 1890s. Her specialty was chain breaking and weightlifting, and it was said she proved "that even that sweetly pretty name could not prevent her from being a strong lady." Here Flossie is given a place of honor in a vaudeville performance in Berlin, New Hampshire, c. 1890.

17. Women wrestlers often gave their audiences a thrill by getting into the ring with men. Here a formidably built lady takes on a strongman. This Austrian postcard from c. 1900 was almost certainly meant to be comic in intent, but it is also erotic. The lady's nipples are visible, and the combat between a man and a woman is clearly a sly reference to the sexual act. The barbells and the other strongmen in the background are there to show the "professional" setting, no doubt to allay threats of censorship.

18. One of the first women to become a true success as a professional strongwoman was Athleta. We only know her married name, Mme. van Huffelen, and that she was born in Antwerp, Belgium, in 1868. Her tours as a "female Hercules" took her all over Europe and America. This photo, c. 1900, shows her to be a powerful presence, but she has concealed her muscles quite effectively, thus rendering her less of a threat to the male members of the audience.

19. This ad appeared in a German vaudeville publication c. 1890. It announces that the strongwoman is, "A headliner for establishments of the first rank! Athleta, the unique, strongest, unsurpassed and fashionable strong lady in modern times." The illustration emphasizes her hips and muscular upper body, and the sketches of parts of her act show an impressive array of stunts.

ATHLETA

M.F.
PARIS

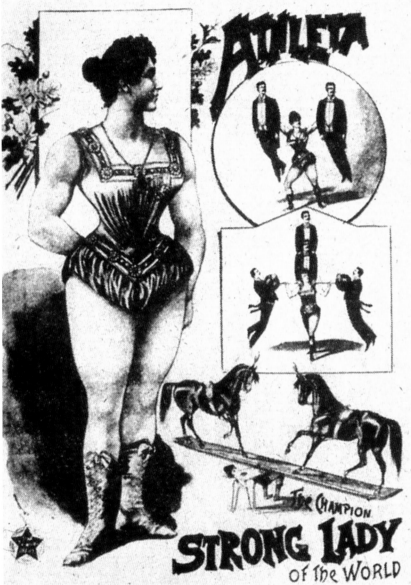

20. This ad from an English trade magazine shows Athleta performing a spectacular horse seesaw stunt. Popular and much imitated, this trick was first devised by theatrical strong-men; only the top acts could afford two trained horses. The lady is in the so-called "Tomb of Hercules" position, with hands back and legs forward, the balancing plank resting on her abdomen.

21. The Belgian strongwoman had figured out that one of the ways that she could amaze audiences was to lift a man on her shoulders. Eventually she was able to support half a dozen burly males as well as an oversized barbell.

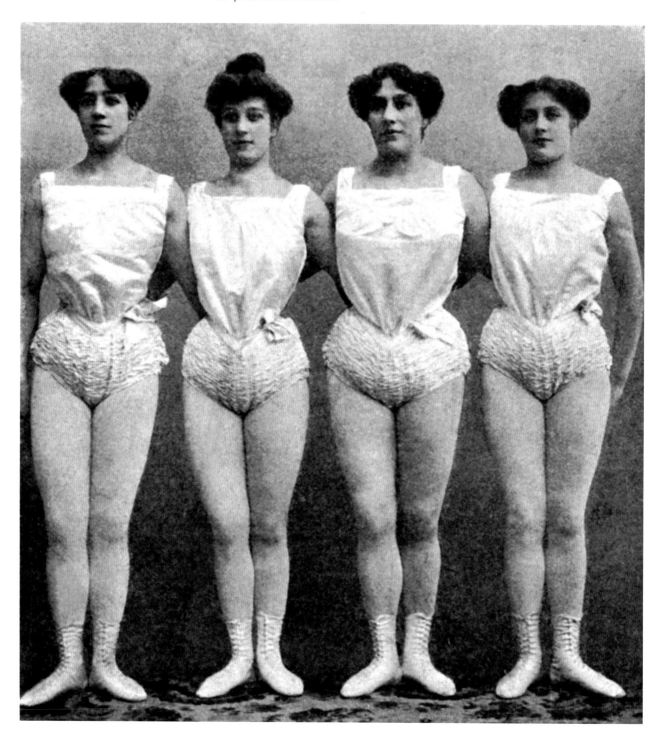

22. Athleta had three daughters whom she brought up to be strongwomen too. Brada, Louise, and Anne (left to right) are shown here in a graceful pose with their mother. The girls never achieved the same fame or glory as Athleta, perhaps because they lacked both her strength and showmanship. It is significant that none of these supposed strongwomen choses to display her muscles in this family portrait—grace and beauty are more in their line.

23. The *Fête foraine* (fun fair or carnival) was one of the most important settings in which athletes could demonstrate their prowess. The company would erect a booth and then try to drum up business by giving the public a little taste of what awaited them inside where the real show was held. This postcard from 1909 depicts the parade of athletes. In this case, a strongwoman in the troupe, Jeanne Gillot, could be counted on to titillate the mostly male audience and dangle the possibility of seeing something risqué.

24. Most carnival strongwomen performed anonymously, but we know the name of Jeanne
Gillot. She lifted weights and even wrestled with men or other ladies, as circumstances required.
She was apparently as strong as she was adroit, and many a male opponent who decided that
he could wrestle her into submission was forced to admit that a girl beat him.

25. A carnival wrestler who called himself Marseille operated this booth in the early twentieth century. He realized that the sight of a bit of feminine leg, as well as a chance to see the novel Japanese sport of "Jiu-Jitsu," would help to drum up a large crowd.

26. Indian clubs were large, wooden bowling pin-shaped devices that were swung in various routines in order to develop strength and dexterity. This pretty but anonymous young lady posed with her clubs for a photograph in Denver, Colorado, c. 1890. Her fancy costume and undeniable poise before the camera suggest that she may have been a professional vaude-ville *artiste*.

27. The great French poster artist Jules Chéret created this magnificent work in 1880, showing one of the most remarkable female strength per-formers of the time. Born in 1858 in Stettin, Poland, Miss Lala was the child of a black father and a white mother. She was very muscular, and more than one man was reportedly jealous of her large biceps. This depiction captures her most spectacular stunt: hanging from a trapeze while grasping a can-non in her jaws. The cannon was then fired as she bit down on a connecting chain.

28. "A lady who practices the sports of strength" is the only identification given to this French photo c. 1890. She was posed like a Herculean male with her arms folded across her chest, thereby emphasizing her hips and legs.

29. Madame Herculine was a music hall weightlifter. She probably specialized in harness lifting because she has a rope looped over her neck; with this, she would pick heavy objects off the floor using complicated scaffolding. Any time there was an elaborate device involved, the chances for chicanery increased exponentially. Her elaborate costume is certainly fetching, but this too meant that many aids to her lifting could be concealed beneath the folds. Herculine was probably a charlatan, but a pretty and entertaining one.

30. In the early twentieth century, nothing conveyed the modern spirit of mobility, freedom, and independence better than the bicycle. When a pretty athletic girl was included, she added sexual desirability to the mix—a sleek human machine joined to the manufactured machine. To many observers, this novel combination was exciting and perhaps a little frightening.

31. The close-cropped hair, pose emphasizing strength, and formidable barbells and kettlebells all give this anonymous strongwoman a masculine air, but her frilly, lacy costume keeps her in the realm of the feminine. The melancholy expression on her face, either from the strain of a long exposure time or some secret sorrow, gives this image an added poignancy. American photograph c. 1890.

32. This odd Russian postcard dates from just before the October Revolution of 1905, and combines an intriguing mixture of female strength, sexuality, and anti-capitalist propaganda. The "Rehearsing Star" here is obviously a professional athlete since she is surrounded by her weights. She holds aloft a rich admirer who grasps a bag of money in his hands (presumably to lure the woman into his clutches), but the woman's pointing finger reveals the man's real intentions as well as the lady's knowledge of them.

33. Women have often served as beautiful props for strongmen, and in this German postcard c. 1900 a male athlete holds in his hand a lovely but hardly sylph-like beauty. (The Victorians liked their ladies to be more physically substantial than modern ideals.) The image also implies that the man holds the woman in his hands and thus can control her, although this woman's sheer bulk seems to indicate otherwise.

34. The four Clementinos were a group of acrobats who performed in the first decades of the twentieth century; their greatest claim to fame was using a very powerful woman as their understander. She is shown in this advertising postcard in the central vignette supporting the three other members with her powerful shoulders and arms. The fact that they are waving American flags means very little in terms of their nationality; names and origins changed frequently in the world of professional athletes.

35. "This young man will wrestle with the lady! Wrrrestling! Wrrrestling!" shouts the carnival tout. The fact that the "young man" is not exactly in the first bloom of youth (nor is his opponent) and the pathetic appearance of the others gives it a partly humorous, partly tawdry quality. The sad and threadbare world of the carnival is thus revealed in this German postcard from the first decade of the twentieth century.

36. It is very difficult to imagine the delicate little mademoiselle in this French photograph bending an iron rod, so perhaps the stunt was faked. The curve of her body mimics the curve of the bar in her hands, and the purpose of the photo might simply have been to display her legs and slender figure. Image c. 1900.

37. Elvira Sepisvort was either a professional wrestler or strongwoman from Estonia, and she clearly had a powerful, bulky physique. Estonians valued the physical strength of both their men and women. This real "real photo" postcard is c. 1910.

38. Parisian photographer Lucien Waléry took this image of a girl from the Folies Bergère. The only name given for her is Geezy (a diminutive of Giselle). She was apparently much admired for her athletic physique in turn-of-the-century France, but it is her amazingly elaborate costume that is most on display here. She bats a birdie with her badminton racket, perhaps highlighting her ability to knock men's hearts around.

39. Buffalo Bill was one of the most popular entertainers of the nineteenth century. His Wild West Show introduced thousands of fans to the glories of the American West. Attached to the show was an even larger sideshow, and there, among the other freaks and human curiosities, was Anna, the Physical Culture Girl. This photo was taken in New York c. 1895; she is shown with some of her weights, wearing a very unbecoming outfit.

40. Miss Plaston was a well-known acrobat and strongwoman. In this photo from around 1910, she was posed against a column attempting to look wistful and classical. Miss P. flexed none of her muscles (though she was very strong); instead, she preferred to display her feminine charms by referencing the calm, cool statues of the ancients. Imitating statues was a common technique in the early years of physical culture for both men and women.

L'EFFORT

Mesdames, Messieurs, en attendant le poids de cent kilos, v'la toujours le pois de senteur

161

41. The street-corner strongwoman was satirized in this French postcard from the early twentieth century. "Ladies and gentlemen," she announces, "while waiting for the 100 kilo weight, I can always give you a heavy scent." Strong, muscular women had long been targets of satire, and this card used a particularly earthy humor to poke fun at performers who probably got very little respect in the first place.

42. The Leandros were specialists in *Kraftakrobatik*, or strength acrobatics. There were many variety-show artists who had similar acts, but this Belgian duo was different from most because it was the woman who was the understander rather than the man. This "wonder of female strength" thrilled and amazed audiences all over Europe in the first years of the twentieth century.

43. Gertrude Leandros was born in Antwerp in 1882, the daughter of a professional strongman. A contemporary commentator noted that she "is particularly remarkable for the development of her arms, deltoids and legs." Her partner and later husband (alas, no name has survived) was no slouch himself. The couple posed for this photo c. 1900.

44. A less successful version of the Leandros was the British husband-and-wife team of Marguerite and Hanley. They attempted much the same thing as their Belgian colleagues, but with less artistry and acclaim. Still, the sight of a woman who could lift and balance a man was always a curiosity.

45. Grete Wolfram was a "prize-winning lady athlete and club swinger." In this photo c. 1900 she holds the club close to her face in a way that might have some sadomasochistic overtones. Was Fräulein Wolfram trying to appear both seductive and dangerous at the same time?

46. An animal skin, a heavy iron weight, and a huge club studded with brass nails and strips of metal are the props in this photograph of Grete Wolfram. In addition to being a championship club swinger, she was an Austro-German record holder in weightlifting, but here her athleticism was portrayed in a kittenish rather than a sporting pose.

47. Photographer C.L. Weed of Detroit, Michigan, took this evocative photo of Madam Duboise, Lady Samson, c. 1885. She wears a corsage to draw our attention to her breasts and a wide sash to bring our eyes to her narrow waist. Her short skirt might well have been too daring for Detroit, so perhaps the very distracting garden fence served to shield her from the viewer's gaze.

48. Bag punching was not an activity that many women indulged in around 1895 when this photograph was taken. It was the reserve of male pugs and grapplers, and the fact that the lady in the picture is posed this way is slightly daring. She wears a very formfitting jersey and tights, indicating that she might not have been a "lady" at all.

49. French-Canadian athlete Louis Cyr was almost certainly the world's strongest man when this was taken in 1889. Cyr, his little daughter, and his wife Mélina are shown in this charming family photo. The diminutive Mélina was part of her husband's strength act. She had a sturdy, slim figure, and she not averse to showing it off.

50. Kate Roberts, born in 1883, was one of the most successful music hall strongwomen of the early twentieth century. She was strong, muscular, feminine, and beautiful—an irresistible package for Edwardian theatergoers. Under her redoubtable stage name of Vulcana, she thrilled audiences with her strength and poise.

51. If there were any doubts that Vulcana was muscular, one had only to take a look at her guns. Many men wished they had muscles this big. She was reportedly the daughter of an Irish minister living in Wales, but this may have been a complete fiction, since many performers invented very creative autobiographies for themselves. That she was both strong and beautiful is evident.

Vulcana, World's Greatest Lady Athlete

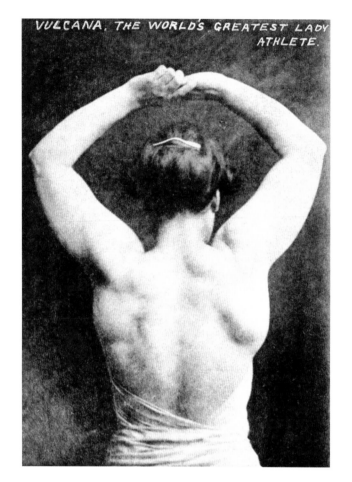

VULCANA, THE WORLD'S GREATEST LADY ATHLETE.

52. Vulcana's back muscles are extraordinarily well-developed. Even more unusual is the fact that she had herself photographed in such a state of undress. This was seriously hot stuff in the early 1900s.

53. Vulcana's act consisted of strength feats in which she lifted both large weights, as shown here, and full-grown men. One contemporary commentator remarked that "she has the biceps and shoulders of a man, but her legs and hips are without a doubt those of a woman."

54. Vulcana performed in the variety theaters of Great Britain and the continent with her "brother" (shown here), a strongman who called himself Atlas. The two were actually husband and wife, but why disappoint all those avid ticket-buying stage-door johnnies?

55. Although it was as a fearless lion tamer that Claire Heliot (1866–1959) achieved great fame and fortune, she was clearly quite strong. In 1902, the German entertainer took her act to the Hippodrome in London, and she became an immediate sensation. Here she appears on the cover of Britain's premier muscle magazine carrying a 360-pound lion named Sascha. Heliot (whose real name was Clara Pleßke) chose to perform in elegant gowns, emphasizing her femininity and vulnerability (although she was anything but helpless). She preferred the company of her lions and (it is said) other women to married thralldom. "I could have married several times," she claimed, "but I have too strong a will to be subordinated by a man."

56. The first two decades of the twentieth century were a golden age for female strength performers, and among the best of these was Elvira Sansoni. She started out performing with a partner around 1891, but by 1901 when this poster was published, she had begun a solo act. The bubbles in this illustration show some of her lifting stunts, including many of the spectacular (but often faked) tricks of other strongwomen. It was her petite figure and flower-like beauty that made her more memorable than many others.

HEALTH IS THE BEST WEALTH.

HEALTH & STRENGTH

2d.

March, 1902.

Vol. iv.   No. 3.

CLAIRE HELIOT CARRYING A FULL-GROWN LION.

AS SEEN AT THE LONDON HIPPODROME.

MISS ELLA,
OF THE
SCHIAVONI TROUPE
The
**STRONGEST
WOMAN**
IN THE
WORLD.

MISS ELLA,
OF THE
SCHIAVONI TROUPE.
THE
STRONGEST
WOMAN IN THE
WORLD.

57. No one knows what Elvira Sansoni's real name was, but we do know that she was born in Germany sometime around 1870. Her close-cropped coiffeur gives her a certain androgynous appeal, which is in contrast to her demure, girlish pose. In her day, Sansoni was known as "the greatest female Hercules of modern times." Today poor Elvira is as forgotten as Ozymandias.

58 *(above)*. The Schiavoni Troupe was a vaudeville acrobatic group that toured North America in the 1910s. They were good enough to have been filmed by the Pathé company in France in 1913. Miss Ella was a member, and she is advertised here as "the strongest woman in the world." She was no such thing, but she did have impressive biceps, and she was not afraid to show them.

59 *(left)*. In addition to being acrobats, the Schiavonis also had a "posturing act", that is, they posed in imitation of classical statues. Here Miss Ella mounts a revolving pedestal and shows off her triceps. This is an unusual pose for a woman of her time to assume. Miss Ella may be one of the true pioneers of women's bodybuilding.

60. Another great English strong-woman from the golden age was Athelda. Her real name was Frances Rheinlander; she was born in Manchester, UK, but little else is known about her. She was posed for this photograph in a typically masculine attitude with her impressive arm flexed and her leg advanced forcefully.

61. This poster from 1914 shows that Athelda was enough of a showperson to realize that good photos and attractive posters could boost the evening's take. It is interesting that the largest photo is of Athelda's lovely naked back and seductive gluteal hemispheres, thus showing that she was using her sex appeal as well as her unusual strength to draw in the public.

KYRLE PICTURE PALACE,
GLOUCESTER ROAD, ROSS.

Commencing February 22nd, 1915, and during the week, Flying Visit of

ATHELDA
THE GREAT.

Miniature
LADY HERCULES,
Britain's
Beautiful Daughter.

Part 1. Physical Culture.
Part 2. Science & Strength.

GRAND WEIGHT LIFTING COMPETITIONS,
Commencing Wednesday Evening,

When Prizes will be given for the best attempt.   All competitors must be over 17 years of age.   Competitors are competing amongst themselves and not against ATHELDA the great, but she will act as judge.

Concertina Competitions Monday & Tuesday.   **Competitors to bring their own Instruments.**

SPECIAL STAR PICTURES THIS WEEK.

FRIDAY NIGHT SINGING COMPETITION.

DORIS YOUNG, Child Vocalist.   VEDA OLIVE, Chic Comedienne, Of the Principal Music Halls.

T. R. CHINN, From London and Leading Halls. in his great Concertina Act of Harmony and Humour.

Introducing his own invention, the Split Instrument, also the smallest and largest Concertinas made to the value of £120.

Times and Prices as usual.   Free list entirely suspended.

62. Muscular poses of a reclining model, whether male or female, are rare because they are difficult to do successfully, but Athelda acquits herself well in this photograph c. 1910. She flexes both her biceps and her triceps in this posture and is also able to display greater expanses of flesh than most female performers of the day.

63. Luise (or Louise) Leers was born around 1907 in Wiesbaden, Germany; her trapeze artist father taught her how to thrill circus audiences around the world. In this photo, the "trapeze phenomenon" flexes her shoulder and arm muscles (which show the well-developed musculature typical of an acrobat) while the large ribbon in her hair, conversely, makes her look girlish and innocent. It is an excellent representation of the balance that muscular women had to maintain until very recently.

64. In the 1920s, Leers was brought to America where she performed in the Ringling Brothers and Barnum & Bailey Circus. She became famous for her "giant revolutions," or one-arm swings in which she threw her entire body in a circle while grasping a rope high above the ring. At the height of her strength she could perform 190 revolutions in a row. No wonder her back and arm muscles are spectacularly developed.

65. Anna Anthonius was a Finnish wrestler from the first decade of the twentieth century. Little is known of her beyond her participation in a few tournaments in Germany and northern Europe. There was a vogue for female wrestling in the early 1900s; before World War I, troupes of women athletes crisscrossed Europe giving wrestling exhibitions, but (as with much professional wrestling) many of these were closer to entertainment than sporting events. Women's wrestling was revived in North America in the 1940s and '50s.

66. Charmion was something of a force of nature in the first decade of the twentieth century. She was a strongwoman, trapeze artist, and first-class self-promoter who handed out celluloid pinback buttons like these. (The photographer was Frederick W. Glasier; the Hyatt Manufacturing Company of Baltimore, Maryland produced the buttons c. 1900.) In addition to showing off her impressive musculature (a rare occurrence in itself), the Sacramento-born performer reveals a scene from her most infamous showpiece, the "Trapeze Disrobing Act." In this act, she would sweep onto the stage in an elaborate gown and a stylish plumed hat, jump up on the trapeze, and then systematically remove one article of clothing after another until she had arrived as close to nudity as the laws of the time would permit. She then flexed her muscles and displayed her considerable arm and shoulder development. Thomas Edison was so impressed that he filmed her performing this routine in November of 1901.

67. Another strongwoman who used pinback buttons was Texie. In fact, she may have been the first to display her image in this way, as the date on the back of this pin is 1896. Nothing is known of the subject, but by proudly flexing her biceps, Texie puts herself in a rare group of early performers who show off their strength and muscularity.

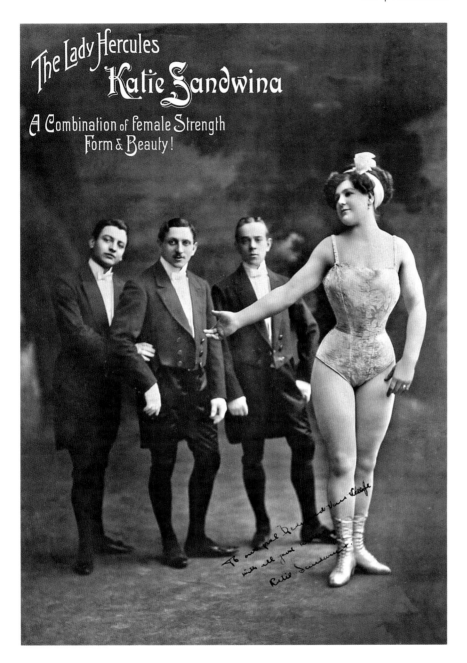

68. The strongest and most famous strongwoman of the Golden Age of the early twentieth century was Sandwina. Her birth name was Katie Brumbach. She stood over six feet tall and had enough bulk and muscle to amaze audiences with her prowess. Sandwina came from an athletic family, and in this poster c. 1900 she lifts three people (probably siblings) on a bicycle.

69. Sandwina was always promoted as a paragon of both female strength and beauty. She might have been extraordinarily strong, but always emphasized that she was also sweet, charming, and, above all, feminine. Here the shapely strongwoman points to her husband and her two sons as if to show us that she is a wife, mother, and one-hundred percent woman. The photo was taken c. 1915.

70. Sometime around 1900, Kate Brumbach married Max Heymann, and he became her manager and occasional co-star. Sandwina's huge stature was emphasized in this photo with her shorter husband.

71. Sandwina toured for many seasons with the Barnum & Bailey Circus during the 1910s and '20s, and as was the trend, she always made a point of lifting a man (here, it is her husband, Max). In the background is their son Ted, who later became a heavyweight boxer.

72. Sandwina lifts two circus supernumeraries in this photograph c. 1920. There were many pictures of Sandwina lifting things and people, but not a single photo has survived showing the woman flexing her muscles. That would have diminished her femininity, and she would never allow even the slightest diminution of her image as a perfect woman, as opposed to a perfect athlete.

73. The Braselly Sisters were a pair of strongwomen who specialized in graceful and artistic strength stunts. They were also sisters of the even more famous female athlete, Sandwina. Here the two ladies do an adagio (acrobatic balancing) act. The photo found its way into *The Police Gazette* in 1909 where it was titled "Muscles and Music." The editors asked rhetorically, "But don't you think the lady athletes are a stunning pair of statuesque beauties?"

74. Professional strongman Eugen Sandow started one of the earliest physical culture magazines; in the first decade of the twentieth century it was one of the most popular sporting
publications in Britain. *Sandow's Magazine* used a clever mixture of health, fitness, and scantily
clad models (male and female) to attract readers. Here is a case in point. It is perhaps the first
swimsuit issue of a sports magazine, dated May 1906. "La Milo" was actually an "actress" (or a
pinup girl) known for her poses as a "Water Nymph." Her real name was Pansy Montague; she
was born in Sydney, Australia.

75. In 1906 a successful musical revue called *The Dairymaids* was playing on the London
stage, and its most famous set piece was this scene that took place in the gymnasium of Miss
Penelope Pyechase's academy. The producers were taking advantage of the women's physical culture craze that had swept Europe and North America, and in this elaborate setting, the
chorus girls all participated in various athletic activities.

76. Carrie Moore, the star of *The Dairymaids*, pretends to lift a large barbell in this hand-tinted postcard from 1906. Her tightly fitting costume was perhaps the real reason for her success in this production.

77. The most famous song from the otherwise forgettable *Dairymaids* is "The Sandow Girl," which was performed by an Australian actress named Carrie Moore (shown facing the camera in the top photo). Eugen Sandow was the most reknowned strongman and gymnasium owner in the world, so his name was immediately recognizable to the audiences of the time. Several other girls in the number mimed weightlifting and strand pulling, but it was their tightly fitted long dresses that left very little to the imagination that made the scene so successful. Another Sandow Girl, Miss Maude Odell, admired herself in the mirror.

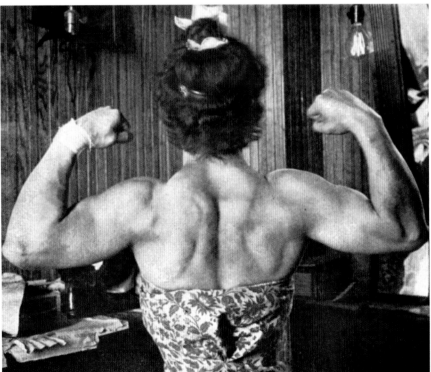

78. *The Dairymaids* was such a resounding success that it ran for 239 performances before moving to New York, Sydney, Australia, and then back to London. The last recorded performances occurred in 1915, long after its original run. The show made a star of Carrie Moore, and in this photograph she took advantage of her fame to advertise Majestic Manicure Paste.

79. Luisa Picchiani was an Italian acrobat who performed in America with a troupe of eight performing "sisters" (two of whom turned out to be boys in drag). This was a common occurrence in acrobatic troupes. Seventeen-year-old Luisa, however, was a real girl. Arms are flexed proudly for this photograph and the one of her sister (below) that appeared in a 1902 issue of *Frank Leslie's Weekly*.

80. Polissena Picchiani was the strongest of the acrobatic siblings from Italy, and it was said that she had "biceps like [strongman Eugen] Sandow." Her back and shoulders also show impressive development.

81. Professor Louis Attila was an established fitness and bodybuilding instructor who had a famous gymnasium on Times Square in New York City. He trained many important strongmen, including Eugen Sandow himself. He was also very interested in women's exercise. Caroline Baumann was perhaps his most successful female pupil, and she is shown here around 1910. Baumann later became an instructor at Attila's gymnasium; she also performed briefly in her own strongwoman show on vaudeville.

82. The Collin Troupe were gymnasts who performed in continental Europe in the first decade of the twentieth century. Acrobatic troupes at this time almost always included at least a few women. They spiced up the act, gave it some glamour, but they usually did not steal the athletic thunder from the real stars: the men. The women in this photo, c. 1905 in Berlin, shows two fit and athletic-looking girls, but the muscular men behind them did most of the acrobatic work. The man in the center, known only as Krono, was the strongest of the group.

83. This professional strongwoman demonstrated the problem that affected oversized, powerful women: how can one be strong but feminine at the same time? Amanda Klimunt would never be described as delicate, yet she did her best to adopt a graceful pose by averting her gaze and daintily lifting the edges of her cloak.

84. There are no clues in this photograph to tell us where it was taken; it shows a professional strongwoman doing a common stunt, a back lift. Huge weights (here about a dozen men) would be placed on a plank, and the athlete would then get beneath and raise the plank on her back. It was a spectacular feat that never failed to please audiences. From the men's clothing, it would appear that this picture was taken c. 1920.

Amanda Klimunt,
Salon-Athletin
Gruß aus Zirkus Raphael.

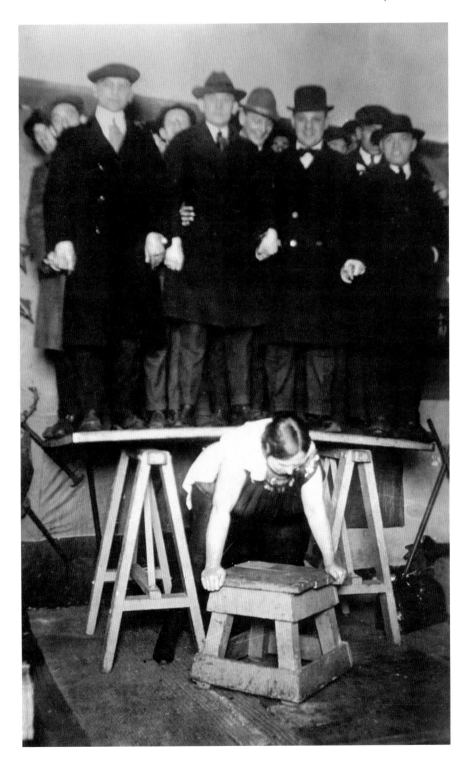

85. A sinewy back and arms knotted with muscles are the marks of an acrobat. Regina Floria was an Anglo-Italian circus gymnast and trapeze artist in the 1920s and '30s. Her father was a music hall strongman named Luigi Borra, so Regina was raised around athletes.

86. Ewald Redam (at far left) was the principal athlete in a troupe of German strength performers who were active in the 1920s. During World War I, Ewald, his Latvian wife Ludmilla, and two other athletes formed the Four Redams. Their act was a great hit, even more remarkable because the women got as much attention for their strength feats as the men. In the 1930s, the group added two more strong women.

87. An anonymous English strong-woman flexes her arms as she holds a fake sword above her head. The photograph was taken in the late 1920s in Manchester, England, the lady was probably an acrobat of some sort.

88. Another British athlete flexes her shoulders and arms in this impressive back pose. Her fancy costume indicates that she was involved in show business, most probably as an acrobat. Photo by B.L. Pearson of Manchester, England.

89. In the Hellwegh-Bella team of acrobats from Germany, the man's muscularity is contrasted with the beauty
and grace of the woman's body. The
photograph is c. 1920s.

90. Mr. L. and Mrs. P. Neser were
professional athletes from the town of
Ludwigshafen am Rhein in Germany.
Here they display the most common
way of using a woman in a vaudeville
act: she was something to lift, throw,
or project through the air, an ornament
in tights, but seldom the star of the
turn.

91. June Perlane reversed the
traditional gender order by lifting a
man into the air. This feat had been
a favorite of strongwomen, but with
the decline of vaudeville in the 1920s
and '30s, fewer women attempted it.
La Perlane continued the tradition in
North America with this lift.

92. Romulo and Betty had a strength act which they displayed all over central Europe in the years between the wars. Betty represents grace and beauty while Romulo is there for the raw strength that a man brings to an act of this sort.

93. Marta Farra was a professional strongwoman. She was also one of the most unrepentant charlatans in theatrical history. In this photo, the diminutive German girl appeared to lift an elephant in a "harness lift" in the middle of New York's Times Square in April of 1924. Any time an elaborate device such as this one is used, one could be almost certain that trickery, not real strength, was involved in the lifting of heavy objects.

94. Aerialist and strongwoman Lillian
Leitzel was one of the most glamorous and popular entertainers in the
Ringling Brothers and Barnum & Bailey
Circus. Her specialty was doing a
series of hundreds of one-armed flips
on a taut rope; she would momentarily
dislocate her shoulder during each flip.
Because of her talent, strength, and diminutive beauty, the public adored her.
Unfortunately, she was reputed to have
a highly volatile temper and infused her
private life with just as much drama as
her circus performances. This poster
is c. 1930.

PUMPING WOOD

Obviously, not all muscular women were professional strongwomen, acrobats, or variety-stage performers, as portrayed in the last chapter. This chapter will explore the women (including female athletes) who merely wanted to stay reasonably strong and fit through exercise and physical culture. Many wondered how they should go about this task, and how strong was strong enough. One of the main reasons that professional strongwomen could make a living was because they were assumed to be rarities among members of the "weaker sex." In the nineteenth century, exercise was thought to put the health, vigor, and femininity of *ladies* in deadly peril.

A constant theme that ran through early women's physical culture literature was that females were generally frail and delicate creatures, lovely but fragile flowers who would wilt if taken outside of their protective hothouse. Decent women were supposed to be trussed up in corsets and tight lacing, smothered under yards of undergarments, and swathed in long, heavy skirts—all of which were balanced atop dainty, high-buttoned shoes. No wonder many nineteenth- and early twentieth-century women avoided exercise.

Starting in the mid-1800s, however, a new philosophy began to be promulgated. Pioneers such as Friedrich GutsMuths, Phokion H. Clias, and Diocletian Lewis declared that women ought to exercise regularly. If nothing else, physical activity would make them stronger for the ordeal of childbirth and housework. Many of these workouts were little more than arm waving and calisthenics, as heavy exercise was considered dangerous for women's delicate constitutions; most early advocates of female physical culture advised their students to grasp

95–97. By the first quarter of the nineteenth century, many educational authorities agreed that some sort of physical activity was good for women. An article in *Harper's Weekly* from 1857 laments "the short duration of the health and beauty of American ladies," but published a series of exercises that were designed to improve the situation. The first recommends push-ups against a chair back; the second shows how to "pump wood" (since the dumbbells in the illustration are made of it); and the last one shows how to hang from a doorway. "The physical deterioration of the Americans as a people is remarked upon by almost every traveler who comes among us," the article presciently warns.

only light beanbags, books, or wooden dumbbells in their hands as they swung their arms.

Many women enjoyed the new vigor and well-being that even these moderate exercises engendered, and they soon discovered that they could lift heavier objects than the piddly wooden dumbbells they'd been restricted to. Few of the women who exercised, either with weights or without, were interested in building muscular physiques. They sought health and beauty; muscularity was not seen as a viable goal. Professional strongwomen or sinewy acrobats might revel in their muscularity, but the vast majority of ordinary women merely wanted to correct an orthopedic condition, stay fit and healthy, or retain their girlish figures as long as possible.

There were a number of ailments that fashionable women suffered from at the time; many are now thought to have been side-effects of wearing tightly laced corsets. These constricted the female midsection to absurdly narrow dimensions, thus dislodging internal organs, pinching the lungs, and leaving the wearer short of breath and partially immobile. The purpose of corsets, of course, was to make the breasts and hips look larger. Unfortunately, the price for trussing oneself up in such a device was high. Exercise was made doubly difficult, and the resulting debilitation was increased. In some of the early exercise photos and drawings, the women are clearly wearing their corsets while they go through their movements, as it was considered indecent to unlace in public.

As the twentieth century began, a new idea entered the discourse of exercise, which suggested that a strong and healthy woman was an independent woman, and she might reflect a new social freedom. A woman could be strong and even muscular and still be feminine and seductive. Once women had tasted physical power, they often yearned for political power, too. Unfortunately for social conservatives, the reverse was also true: the desire for political strength sometimes engendered a taste for physical strength. As some men found, to their cost, the hand that rocks the cradle may rule the world, but the muscular female arm that wields a dumbbell (or a menacing rolling pin) can threaten male domination.

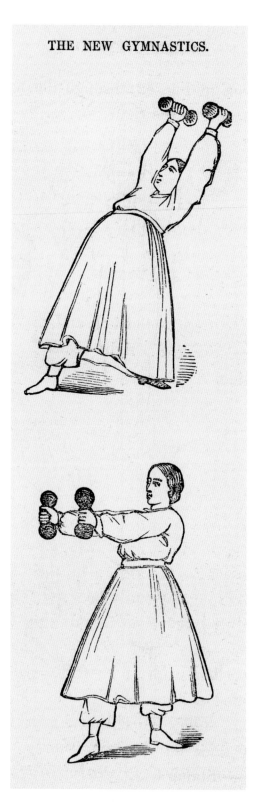

THE NEW GYMNASTICS.

Seaside Belles.
Copyright 1897, by Strohmeyer & Wyman.

98. An American gymnastics teacher with the unlikely Roman name of Diocletian (or Dio) Lewis was worried about women's health and strength issues. He felt that women as well as men could benefit from physical exercise, and in his book *The New Gymnastics*, first published in 1862, he made the radical and daring suggestion that women should wear bloomers to facilitate movement during exercise.

99. Dio Lewis thought that ladies should exercise with dumbbells, albeit of the light, wooden variety; he suggested this exercise in which the woman stamps her foot, rears back, and lifts her dumbbells, then brings them forward. This was not intended to build muscles, but it was a first step to acclimatizing females to using weights and other muscle-building devices.

100. "Seaside Belles" is the subject of this stereoview showing a bit of nineteenth-century cheesecake. It indicates about as much of the female anatomy as a nice girl would dare to show in 1897 when the photograph was taken. That the ladies are young, fit, and healthy is apparent, but one of the models also seems to be flexing her arm. If she is attempting to show off her muscles, it is a remarkable record of something that very few Victorian girls did.

101. Transforming strong, fit women into objects of lust has been a tried and true method of calming masculine anxieties for ages. Here is a wonderfully smarmy case in point from the *Police Gazette* entitled "Sylphs of the Gymnasium," from 1895; it shows that T&A has a long but not very noble pedigree.

102. This group of earnest female athletes was photographed sometime in the 1880s in Milwaukee, Wisconsin; they are in their workout togs and some have laid Indian clubs on the floor in front of them. It is most likely that they were part of a Sokol, or Czech gymnastics society. The gentleman in the back row was undoubtedly their instructor, and the other young man (third from left) is probably the brother of one of them. It is his belt buckle that provides the clue to identifying the group; it features the elaborate S that was one of the insignias of the Sokol society.

103. In August of 1872, *The Graphic* of London published this illustration of the "Ladies' class at the German Gymnasium." The girls are shown swinging from rings, working with dumbbells, and resting from work with the heavy wand.

104. The William Madsen Physical Culture Institute of Chicago offered its patients massage, exercise, cold baths, Turkish baths, and even jolts of electricity. In this 1894 view of the Gymnasium for Ladies and Children, prospective customers could see the variety of treatments that were available. The female body was always considered more malleable than the male's; it could be twisted, compressed, or pummeled into a more acceptable form.

105-06. In 1887, Duke's Cigarettes published a series of cards that they slipped into their packets of smokes. This was not out of the ordinary; cigarette cards had been around since 1875, but these featured women doing various gymnastics exercises. Modest women in the 1880s wore blousy, capacious outfits when they went to the gym, not the tights and low-cut tops shown here. And since decent women would never smoke tobacco, the audience for these little gems was undoubtedly men who wanted racy pictures of women doing suggestive exercises, such as the "outside hand vault" and the "forward wheel swing."

OUTSIDE HAND VAULT.

W. DUKE SONS & CO.
THE LARGEST CIGARETTE MANUFACTURERS IN THE WORLD.

following spread:

107. *The New York Illustrated News* specialized in sensational stories filled with just enough sexual innuendo to make young boys quiver with excitement and old boys wink in knowing complicity. "Prof. Attila giving one of his favorite New York pupils some lessons in physical culture so that she may become more powerful and shapely" is a case in point. The lady's lifting form is atrocious, but her abundant hips and braless bosom are displayed magnificently. This issue is dated April 19, 1894.

108. *The New York Herald* was a much more respectable paper, and girls who lifted weights were sufficiently newsworthy in 1899 to warrant several illustrations of Miss Charlotte Dunphy. Only seventeen years old, she was supposedly the daughter of a "West End Avenue millionaire," formerly a "physical wreck," and "on the verge of the grave." But a course of physical exercise enabled her to perform "feats that astonish professionals." Was she a freak, a fluke, or a floozy? Nineteenth-century readers were not quite sure.

109. Exercise clubs were not at all uncommon for young men, but those that included young women were very rare. Here a group of athletes poses proudly in the late 1890s with their wooden dumbbells firmly grasped in their hands. The ladies seem just as earnest as the gentlemen in this British photograph. Encouraged by such things as a growth in leisure time, rising wealth and education levels, and a naturally competitive spirit, nineteenth-century Great Britain became the birthplace of a sporting movement that soon swept across the rest of Europe and North America. As home to this sporting revolution, the United Kingdom was among the first nations to encourage its young people to exercise.

110. If you were a lady living in San Francisco in the late 1880s and you suffered from a sallow complexion and an "insufficiently developed bust," there was hope. You could deliver yourself into the hands of Dr L.C. Harmon. It is not entirely clear from his advertising brochure how one might remedy these problems, but it had something to do with a strict regimen of exercise and the rubbing of a secret compound of herbs and vegetable matter onto the affected region (presumably by the doctor himself).

111. Dr Harmon's brochure shows a series of engravings contrasting the flat and pallid "before" with the rosy, ample-bosomed "after" on the right, proving there was no end to the ways that physical culture and modern science could improve the female form.

GYMNASTICS FOR GIRLS.

112. In 1884, a magnificent International Health Exhibition was held in London in order to point out the triumphs and the challenges to Britain's public health system. The *Illustrated London News* found many piquant scenes to reproduce from this health fair; one of them was an exhibition of girls' gymnastics. The young ladies swing their wooden dumbbells in a mass drill. The nation was starting to wake up to the issue of female health.

113. The American humor magazine *Puck* attacked the issue of female strength and exercise in this very early satire. In 1880, the problem of women who wanted to gain strength and (by extension) self-determination was the real subject of this illustration. There are plenty of ways that ladies can exercise as they go about their household chores. The harried husband at the center of the illustration seems rather aghast at finding himself being used as a vaulting horse.

114. There was some question about what the well-dressed female athlete should wear, but by the early 1900s, when this girl was photographed, it was generally acknowledged that some form of trousers was preferable. In this case, she wears a version of zouave pants that will thoroughly conceal her thighs while allowing more freedom of movement. A balance beam, heavy rope, and well-stocked racks of Indian clubs complete the scene.

KITCHEN CALISTHENICS—SANITARY SUGGESTIONS FOR THE DOMESTIC DEPARTMENT.

115. This "mechanical" postcard was published c. 1910 during the long run of *The Dairymaids* (see Fig. 78). The metal brad allows the Sandow Girl to bend over as she appears to do real exercises.

116. "Ladies, work out with weights!" exclaims the little verse on this French postcard c. 1900. Far from being an exhortation to the athletic life, the poem encourages women to improve their figures: "Ladies, perform this sport (trust me; I do not jest), and with little effort, you will become as big as this in the chest!"

117. When women first began to work out with weights, it was considered dangerous to have them lift anything heavy and so they were given only two- or four-pound wooden dumbbells. The fact that women lifted much heavier objects in the home seems to have escaped most of the men who designed the exercise. Here two cheerful ladies work out in their street clothes in a photograph c. 1910 by Willis T. White.

Vol. III.   AUGUST, 1900.   No. 5

PHYSICAL CULTURE 5¢

WEAKNESS A CRIME   DONT BE A CRIMINAL.

118. This formally arranged group of athletic ladies, each of whom has a pair of wooden dumbbells in her hands, dates c. 1898. The girls, photographed in Mackinaw City, Michigan, were probably part of a gymnastics class; they were clearly proud of their exercise activities. Victorian modesty forbade them from wearing anything but the long skirts and bulky shirtwaists. Like most women of the time, they had to work twice as hard to achieve half as much as men.

119. The magazine *Physical Culture* began publication in 1899, and by 1900, when this issue was published, it had grown in size and importance. Editor, publisher, and principal writer for the magazine, Bernarr Macfadden was deeply interested in female health and exercise, often featuring photos of women on the cover. This one shows a young Edna Tempest with her trusty wooden dumbbells.

Tavola X.

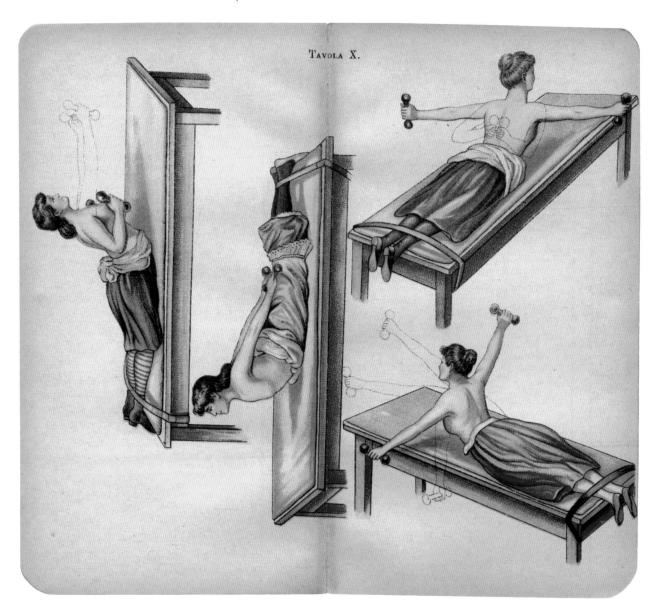

120. Here are some rather bizarre exercises from an Italian book on home fitness. These were described as appropriate for the "special functions" of girls and women who needed to have "a solid pelvis and a well developed abdominal musculature." The model here, most unusually, is topless (although minus her nipples), and she is apparently encouraged to exercise this way. The booklet was published in Turin in 1900.

121. Byrrh billed itself as a "hygienic tonic." It was a fortified wine to which had been added quinine to keep away the scourge of malaria (making it a sort of French alternative to the British gin and tonic). Almost from the start, it was marketed to athletes and those seeking a healthy lifestyle. The company spent a fortune on advertising, and posters extolling the virtues of the concoction were plastered all over Paris. This postcard, c. 1900, was originally one of those posters. Significantly, the parade of athletes includes sporting women reveling in their newly found strength and health.

122. There was considerable specula-
tion about the perfect female form at
the turn of the twentieth century. La
Belle Otéro, a talented Parisian dancer
and courtesan, or *grande horizontale*,
represented one embodiment of physical perfection for audiences of the
1890s. Here she displays her extraordinary figure with its pinched waist,
emphasized by a white bodystocking
contrasted against her black cape.
A figure like this apparently assured
a woman of a parade of *beaux* and
money in the bank.

123. Another version of the perfect
woman is found in the form of this
"fitness model" from the early 1900s.
The corset is gone, and she has a
more natural look. In order to satisfy
nervous censors, however, all of her
naughty bits have been removed. Is
this the first female eunuch?

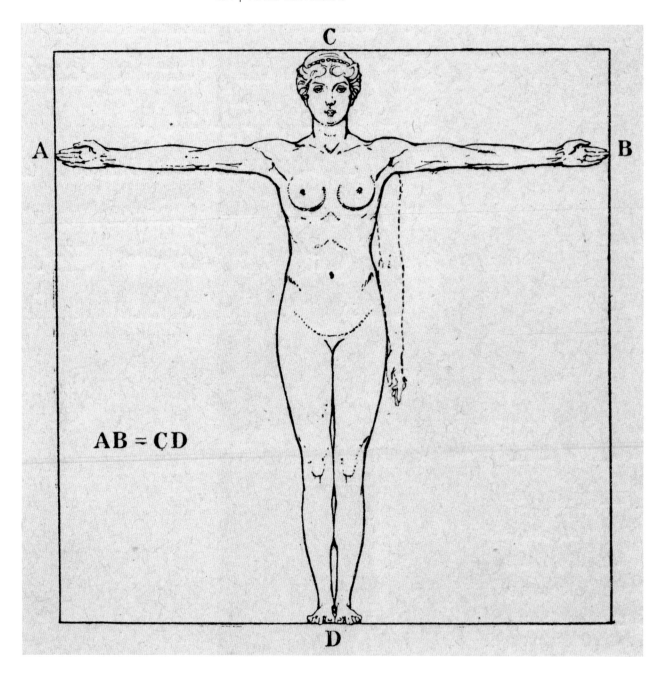

124. As Leonardo da Vinci's Vitruvian Man determined the ideal male, so this drawing attempts to measure the proportions of the perfect female. It was published in Georges Hébert's book *Muscle et beauté plastique* (1919) with the rather prosaic title of *L'envergure* (Stature). The artist is not credited, but he (or she) has here created a simple and beautiful design.

125. By the early 1890s, when this photograph was taken, dumbbells and Indian clubs had spread all the way to Clinton, Iowa, where they were used as props for this studio photo. It is a little unclear whether the young lady in the picture actually used the equipment, but it made her look athletic and modern.

126. The German *Turnverein* (gymnastic) movement began in the early nineteenth century as a response to the defeat of the German states by Napoleon. By 1905, when this postcard was produced, it had morphed into an organization for men and women to exercise and socialize together. The four Fs of the society's motto—*Frisch, fromm, froh, frei* (fresh, reverent, happy, free)—are formed by the bodies of the beer-drinking female gymnasts.

127. The four Fs of the *Turnverein* are visible in the upper left corner of this postcard, c. 1910. The pretty Fräulein in the photo seems to be enjoying her workout with the dumbbells. As World War I approached, preparedness was important on both sides of the conflict.

128. Strong, hefty women have always exhibited an erotic draw for certain men, and the artist of this German postcard from 1910 has apparently taken advantage of that. The puny little man is heaved into the air by a massive Teutonic Valkyrie. The other part of the postcard shows an athletic procession marching through the streets of a German town.

129. The *Turnverein* had its last great meeting before World War I in Leipzig, Germany, in the summer of 1913. Thousands of athletes from all over Europe converged on the city and participated in marches and mass drills. Women athletes had long played an important part in the gymnastics movement; this poster shows a gymnast who seems to brim over with healthy prewar *Gemütlichkeit*.

130. Bathing suits have long been used to show off the figures of athletic ladies, but this potential mermaid is not of the fairy-tale variety. Her smiling face and confident pose lend her a certain charm, however. Wearing a one-piece bathing suit was a rebellious act, as they were illegal in most North American states and provinces. These bathing costumes were often named after their inventor, Annette Kellerman.

131. A trio of shapely ladies in swim-suits poses to show off their trim, athletic bodies. Naturally, bathing cos-tumes (not to mention those wonderful caps) have changed drastically since 1915 when this photo was taken, but the concept of a form-fitting swimsuit is still the same. Of course, it was also important to have an appropriately athletic physique over which one could wear a Kellerman. The world was thus awakening to the importance of sports and exercise in order to look good at the seaside or taking the plunge.

132. Ethel Eldred was clearly a very determined girl. She had her portrait taken about 1905 in her hometown of Detroit, Michigan, wearing a very stylish exercise uniform as she wields a pair of Indian clubs. Her calm but determined expression seems at odds with her gaily decorated and embroidered frock. Was she a club tease?

133. Eugenics was the philosophy, popular early in the twentieth century, that the human gene pool could be improved by selective breeding in which only the fittest and most intelligent humans would be allowed to mate. The movement developed out of the fears of white middle- and upper-class Americans who saw the country as being overrun by physically, intellectually, and racially deficient immigrants from abroad. In this comic postcard c. 1900, a weedy little man sneaks a peek at a genetically superior girl who is working out with weights. The implication is that the little guy is not observing the woman out of any real interest in eugenics at all.

134. Around 1900, it was all the rage to send "vinegar Valentines" that poked vicious fun of people who were easy targets. The female athlete was certainly one of these, and in this example, the verse suggest that athletic girls are vain, ignorant egomaniacs.

135. Of all the vinegar Valentines, this is one of the cruelest, and it ratchets up the campaign against strong women. That such a card was printed and sold shows that many men were clearly worried about strong, independent women. The verse warns the athletic woman: "You can't be a man. Be a lady that's nice. Get a good man by marrying—take my advice."

ATHLETIC GIRL.

You do not follow those books and charts
As much to break heads as you do to break hearts,
Because in your costume you look very fair,
Of which fact you let us all know you're aware.

THE ATHLETIC WOMAN

Jaw like a Jumbo—the Athletic Woman!
  Come on old lady and try to be human;
You can't be a man. Be a lady that's nice,
  Get a good man by marrying—take my advice

COPYRIGHT 1906 BY ARTHUR LIVINGSTON. N.Y 1137

136. Because strong women confused most men, one of the best ways to deal with them was to use a little ridicule. This zaftig girl weightlifter is portrayed with truly Junoesque proportions while the verse implies that she should be spending her time improving her mind, not her muscles.

137. In May 1900, publisher Bernarr Macfadden created *Woman's Physical Development*, the first magazine devoted exclusively to the "cultivation of physical power and beauty in women." The magazine's slogan had a slightly evangelical sound: "Health is beauty. Ugliness a sin." This cover features a very determined-looking but not particularly muscular lady who matched the earnest tone of the magazine.

138. By the time this issue came out three years later, the name of the magazine had been changed (and crossed out on the cover) to *Beauty and Health*. The pretty, smiling girl is much more welcoming and friendly than the young woman on the earlier issue. Macfadden had discovered that most women preferred to be beautiful rather than "physically developed" and healthy rather than strong.

THE ATHLETIC LASS

Oh, the girl who goes in for brawn,
Who's in training from daylight till dawn,
    Should from such stunts refrain
    And develop her brain,
And thank us for "putting her on!"

COPYRIGHT 1905, BY R. HILL

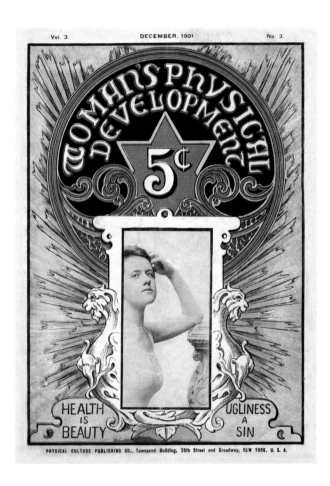

A GYMNASTIQUE

IMP. E HERMET, PARIS.

139. In October of 1905, Bernarr Macfadden decided to organize a Monster Physical Culture Exhibition at New York's Madison Square Garden that would determine the finest male and female physiques. The posters he designed for the show featuring women in skin-tight garments were considered too revealing, and though Macfadden was arrested, the show went on as planned. These photos show the finalists in the women's division. The ladies wore white tights or union suits with a sash around their waists. That photographs like these could have set masculine pulses racing is perhaps surprising to us today, but such was the case.

140. This charming illustration is a trade card published c. 1900 that was handed out to drum up business for a tailor. The girl in this image holds in her outstretched hand a block weight and appears to show very little effort while doing so. At her feet are strewn weights and an Indian club. Her impossibly narrow waist emphasizes her hips and bosom. On the reverse, the pretty young athlete advertises "Le High Life Tailor" in Montmartre, Paris.

141. In 1901, eccentric physical culturist Bernarr Macfadden published *The Power and Beauty of Superb Womanhood*, which covered subjects as diverse as the dangers of corsets, prudishness, and self-abuse. It also presented exercises for developing the body. This topless model in a bizarre pose supposedly illustrates the defects of large ankles and a bust that is too low and "insufficiently developed."

142. Photographs like this one illustrate why Macfadden was often in trouble with censorship authorities. The topless model shows how to perform side bends with arms flexed. One can be almost certain that women were not the only readers of a publication with photos like this in it.

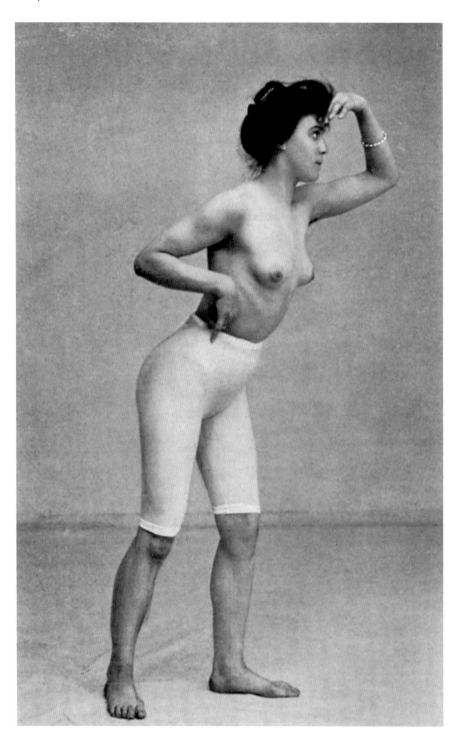

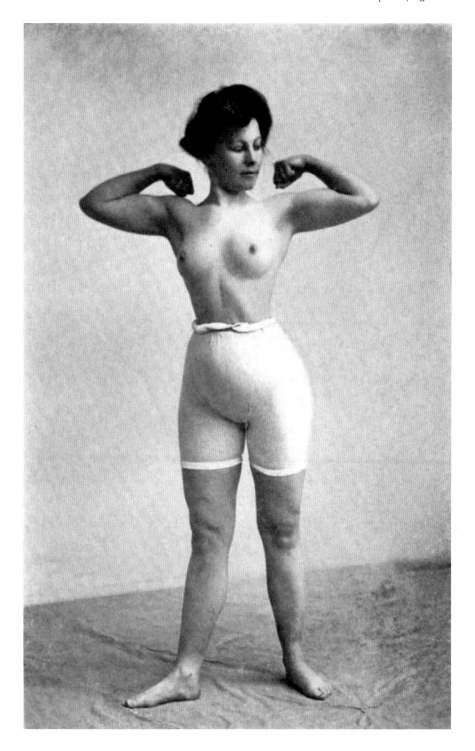

143. The Sokol movement originated in the Czech-speaking regions of the Austro-Hungarian Empire to encourage citizens to exercise and become stronger, healthier, and more nationalistic. Great emphasis was placed on female participation. Every year, mass gymnastics drills involving hundreds of participants were held; this poster advertises one that took place in 1907. The pretty club swinger is meant to exemplify all the finest qualities of her Slavic heritage.

144. Edna Tempest was a real physical culture girl (see also Fig. 119 and 145). She believed in the power of exercise to strengthen a woman's body and to harden her muscles. Tempest married Al Treloar, the winner of the men's competition at Macfadden's great 1905 Physical Culture exhibition. When Treloar later wrote a book called *The Science of Muscular Development*, he used his wife as the female model.

145. Despite her belief in the importance of women's exercise, Edna Tempest advocated very light wooden dumbbells for her female pupils. This was about as effective as waving one's arms around, since a two- or even a four-pound weight offered very little resistance, but it accustomed women to weights and regular, purposive exercise.

146. The Whitely Exerciser was a rubber-strand device that could be attached to the wall in the purchaser's home and used to strengthen the arm and back muscles. By putting a woman on the cover of this advertising brochure from 1901, the makers wanted to emphasize that even females could build muscles with their device. The presence of the animals meant to show that all creatures build their strength and vigor through exercise. Theirs is natural; the modern woman's must be self-determined.

147. Since whips and black silk stockings were not standard equipment in the Sandow system (or any other strength-building program we know about), we may assume that these two ladies are not exclusively interested in exercising. The connection between physical culture and pornography has long been established, but it is seldom as patently clear as in this German photograph c. 1900. Although flogging might be fine exercise, it is highly doubtful that Sandow or Macfadden would have approved (at least in public).

148. Lydia Pinkham marketed a vegetable compound that was supposed to alleviate menstrual and menopausal pains. The company was successful because the remedy was sold by a woman to women at a time when females were considered too childish and emotional to have much medical knowledge. Pinkham's company produced this booklet (with the same title as Bernarr Macfadden's well-known magazine), c. 1900. It featured a female athlete flexing her muscles, and was emblematic of the positive and respectful attitude toward their customers.

149. Many men feared that the logical outcome of allowing women to become independent and physically strong would be women's dominance over men. In this comic postcard from 1909, a "copette" patrols the streets with a rolling pin instead of a nightstick while wearing a fashionable helmet and (perhaps worst of all) a pair of trousers. Her physique recalls those of many female athletes, so the implication is clear: a powerful female body leads quickly to female domination.

150. By 1915, publisher Bernarr Macfadden had learned to be a bit more circumspect about using nude or topless models in his exercise books. This model appears in the book *Vitality Supreme* which appeared in that year, and though she wears a form-fitting exercise costume, everything that is supposed to be concealed is safely hidden from view.

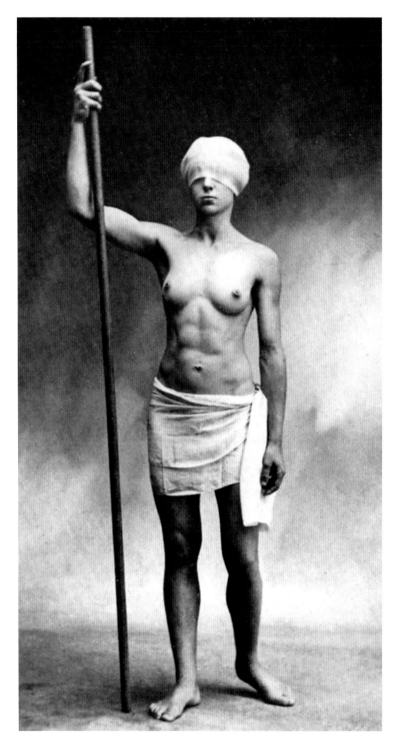

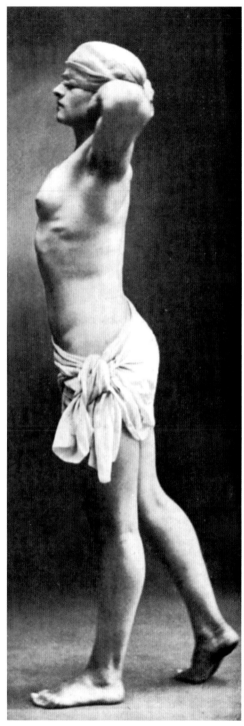

151. Frenchman Georges Hébert published his treatise on women's physical culture in 1919, in which he included this example of a perfectly developed woman. The young athlete was one of the author's pupils, and he remarks in the text that we should admire in particular her arms, abdomen, and legs. Even in France, good girls did not display their naked breasts, so this model has wrapped a scarf around her head to protect her identity.

152. Hébert chose to display the development of the model's abdomen in this photograph from his book on female muscular development.

153. Georges Hébert was an instructor of men's physical culture who advocated a "natural" method. By this he meant that his students must eschew all heavy weights and other "artificial" means of bodybuilding. In 1919 he turned his attention to women and published *Muscle et beauté plastique* (Muscle and Physical Beauty). Developing the students' health and grace were his principal goals, and he had them dress in classical Greek costumes when they were photographed. Here, one of his protégées puts the shot.

154. Hébert often posed his students as classical statues. Here, one of his students adapts the pose of "Diana with a Deer" (minus the deer). Rather than lassoing a forest creature, this Diana is flexing her biceps.

155. "A natural action of throwing with two hands" is the title of this photo, but as interpreted by Georges Hébert it becomes a Grecian fantasy. We are told: "This movement of training the torso is an excellent exercise for the correction of sloping postures. At the same time it forms a pretty image of natural dance." From Hébert's *Muscle et beauté plastique*, 1919.

156. In the 1920s, when Australian swimmer Annette Kellerman published this fitness course, she was already a well-known personality. She had popularized swimming for women, starred in several films, and championed the one-piece bathing costume for women.

PURSUING THE HEALTHY LIFE

By the second decade of the twentieth century, more men and women had a sense of what a strong woman was and how she might achieve even greater strength. Exercise and physical culture helped improve female health and physical power, but women who went to the gym or exercised at home still did it primarily to attain or maintain chic figures. There were wonderful exceptions to the rule, but the twin goals of health and beauty predominated for women in the 1920s and '30s. Real muscularity for women went out of fashion, and because movies were gradually replacing vaudeville as the favorite form of entertainment, fewer and fewer strongwomen appeared in public. New canons of beauty demanded a sleek physique. During World War I, women had driven ambulances, worked in factories, and taken over jobs that were formerly reserved for men. In the postwar era, many women wanted to look more like men, too.

Thanks to the growth of mass media such as magazines and motion pictures, more women were exposed to the new physical ideal. The old hourglass figure was out and so was the S shape of the 1910s; the paragon of beauty was now deemed to be thin, athletic, and peppy. A flat-chested boyish figure became a sign of sexual desirability as well as an indication that one had the means to eat healthily and the leisure time to participate in sport. Dieting and sports became favorite activities for the fashion-conscious, and scales became a must in every woman's bathroom. Health and beauty clubs were widely available to middle-class women for the first time, and having a body attuned to sports and strenuous activity was soon connected in the popular imagination with love, wealth, success, happiness, sexuality, and fulfillment. The new look of the 1920s became emblematic of the freedom that many women felt as they moved in on many of the domains of male-dominated society (sports, work outside the home, and unabashed sexuality). Women's bodies changed accordingly, and the new woman of the 1920s was no longer happy with traditional looks any more than she was with traditional roles. Feminine curves were out, and an androgynous, tomboyish body was in.

Unfortunately, when the Wall Street panic of 1929 caused the stock market to fall, so did hemlines, upraised tennis racquets, and female hopes for greater independence. The onset of the Great Depression in the 1930s meant that many people rushed back to the old, traditional values that were more comfortable in less happy times; they also returned to more traditional expectations for women. This meant that the youthful, boyish flapper was replaced by a more womanly form. In the early thirties, women were expected to go back to old patterns of gender roles; there would be no sexual confusions with the new female body. "The ladylike and stylish look," advised one fashion article in 1931, "no matter how remarkable it may sound in our sports- and outdoor-loving age, is the feminine and fashion ideal of the moment. One must look like a Daughter of Eve and not like the modern Adam!" Girdles and corsets were back in style, and now women exercised to increase their womanly allure; in this they were encouraged by many of their favorite film stars. The movie magazines of the day reported (in excruciating detail) the ups and downs of Greta Garbo's weight and Mae West's bosom.

This was serious business in Hollywood where many of these female stars obsessed constantly over their weight, and many measured out food portions with scientific precision. "One potato, recklessly indulged in," confirmed an article in a 1930 fan magazine, "may cost a contract." Exercise and physical activity still had its place, but only as a tool to make one more attractive. High-kicking chorus girls as well as harried Depression-era housewives wanted to look good for their men. As more of the female body was revealed in photos and films, there was an opportunity for the public to see what the effects of physical training could accomplish. A tall, slender silhouette was considered glamorous, and the slinky evening gowns that wealthier women wore accentuated the long lines and slim waists of the era. A few women at this time also dabbled in nudism, a craze that had spread around the world from Germany, but even if one were not prepared partake in a state of total undress, one could sunbathe and exercise in the open air. A glowing tan was now desirable, and naturally, one's tautly muscled body ought to match the magnificence of one's bronzed and pampered skin.

In the 1930s, a woman with a lightly muscled body could be considered attractive, reflecting the cultural influence of the first female pro athletes such as "Babe" Didrikson Zaharias, golfer Mildred Ella, and tennis star Alice Marble (the first woman to wear shorts at Wimbledon). Building on some of the freedoms of the 1920s, British exercise enthusiast Mary Bagot Stack established the Women's League of Health and Beauty in 1930, which was dedicated to renewing women's energy "in themselves and for themselves." They did this by encouraging women to participate in group gymnastics, dance, and calisthenics—all exercises that were designed to appeal specifically to women, but not so strenuous as to upset traditional gender roles. Toward the end of the 1930s, a new impetus drove many women forward: preparation for global conflict. This was particularly true in Europe where the drums of war began to beat earlier than they did in North America. Many propagandists in dictatorial regimes began to proclaim the glories of the strenuous life. "Modernity means sport," confidently proclaimed one Italian Fascist publication in 1933, "and through all kinds of sports the Fatherland can gain healthy, robust and youthful soldiers and strong mothers." Women were expected to stay strong to keep the home fires burning, make sure that their men were hearty and happy, and give birth to healthy male children who could fight for home and fatherland.

157–58. In 1908, the distinguished Harvard professor of physical culture Dudley A. Sargent declared that Annette Kellerman's figure was perfect because it was just like that of the Venus de Milo. In her seven-volume series of booklets, Kellerman guided women through the travails and mysteries of how they too might become more Venus-like.

THE OLYMPIAN SYSTEM

"Mens sana in corpore sano"

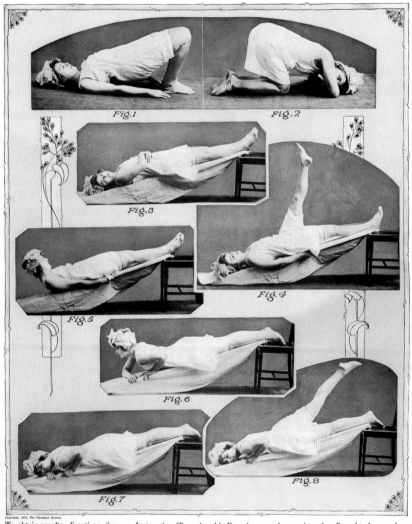

To obtain results, directions given on Instruction Chart for this Exercise must be consistently adhered to by members

CHART C
OVERCOMING WEAKNESSES OF WOMEN

159. In 1919, Bernarr Macfadden was once again at the front of the pack with his "Olympian System," as its appeal was not limited to men. Macfadden realized that women wanted to become fit and healthy too, so he devised a system of simple exercises that could be done in the home, specifically designed for women, i.e., "bosom" exercises and those designed to combat "weakness" (code for menstrual problems). He also created these large posters (thirteen by eighteen-and-a-half inches) with which the exercise routines could be easily followed. This poster provides exercises to address problems due to "weakness and poor circulation." Exercises one through five were supposed to be excellent for pregnant women.

160. Aside from improving one's health, this routine for arms and shoulders was supposed to be "especially desirable for the sake of womanly beauty and general personal attractiveness."

161. The directions on this chart for the development of the bosom state: "A good bust depends primarily upon full chest development, supplemented by active circulation and a healthy state of the glands of the breast."

162. What good is strength if a woman is ungainly, maladroit, or unattractive? Macfadden's copy reinforces this tenant of his exercise philosophy: "In physical training for women the requirements of flexibility, grace and poise outweigh the necessity for unusual strength."

THE
OLYMPIAN SYSTEM
"Mens sana in corpore sano"

Fig. 1 Fig. 2 Fig. 3 Fig. 4 Fig. 5 Fig. 6 Fig. 7 Fig. 8 Fig. 9

To obtain results, directions given on Instruction Chart for this Exercise must be consistently adhered to by members

CHART D
ARMS AND SHOULDERS

THE
OLYMPIAN SYSTEM
"Mens sana in corpore sano"

To obtain results, directions given on Instruction Chart for this Exercise must be consistently adhered to by members

CHART E
BUST AND CHEST DEVELOPMENT

THE
OLYMPIAN SYSTEM
"Mens sana in corpore sano"

To obtain results, directions given on Instruction Chart for this Exercise must be consistently adhered to by members

CHART F
GRACE AND POISE

163. Strand pulling involves spreading rubber or spring expanders apart in order to work the muscles of the upper body. When this photograph was taken in 1931, women had begun to think of their musculature as something that might be built up and strengthened without reducing their overall quotient of femininity.

164. Strand pulling can be a difficult activity, but it builds muscles and tests the mettle of any athlete. This woman is doing a back pull. She uses an expander that has an attached dynamometer, a device to measure and quantify the effort that is needed to pull the strands to their maximum length.

165. By the 1920s, it seemed as if everyone was finding time to exercise. In this photograph, pupils at a French girls' school go through a series of gymnastic drills. The goal of these drills was not muscularity; rather, it was to get a good aerobic workout.

166. Exercise machines have always been popular with those who frequent weight-reduction studios; it is so much easier to wrap a belt around your backside and let it jiggle away the fat than to work up a sweat. Unfortunately, these devices were worse than useless since they would often rattle one's spine out of whack. This cheerful gym enthusiast from the 1920s seems blissfully unaware of the danger (though she does seem to have some problems adjusting the belts).

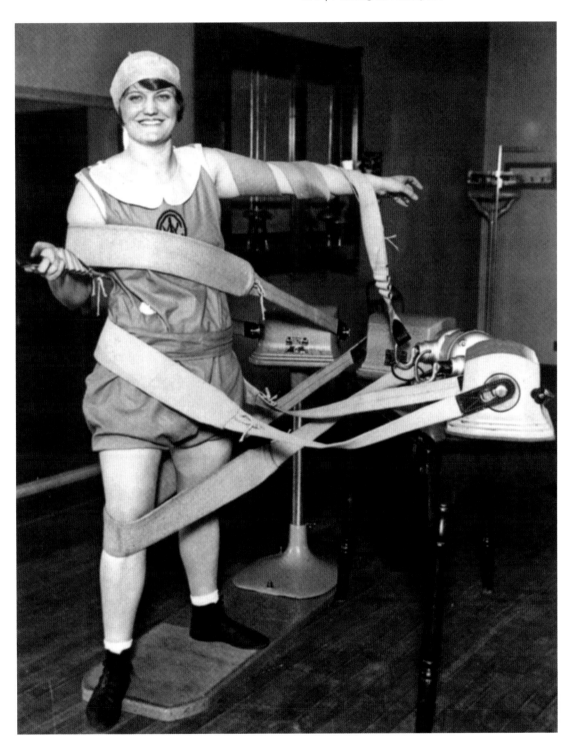

167. Helmar Liederman was a typical beauty queen of the 1920s, and in 1923 the Juneau, Alaska, native entered the Miss America pageant as "Miss Alaska." After she arrived in Atlantic City, it was discovered that officials had forgotten to tell contestants that they had to be single. "Miss" Alaska was not only married to a prominent physical culturist, but she was also a legal resident of New York City. At least she still had her health and a shapely body.

168. By 1926, the Miss America pageant had become enough of a success that Paramount Pictures convinced the organizers to let them make a movie about it. *The American Venus* was the result, and the pretty girls in form-fitting bathing costumes certainly helped to make it a success. Unfortunately, the film itself has been lost, but this wonderful poster remains. It shows the contestants posing gracefully on the beach while Neptune ogles them from the sea.

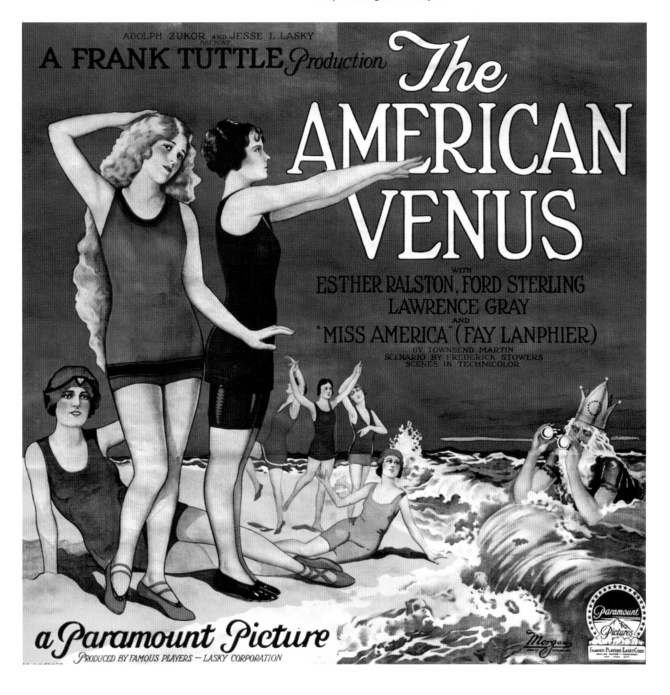

169. "Dainty Marie" Meeker was a circus and vaudeville aerialist who appeared on this cover of *Health and Life* in 1925. She later got into a row with Lillian Leitzel (Fig. 94) who believed that Marie's act, which featured "evolutions on the flying hoops," was too similar to her own. Dainty Marie lost, and left the circus.

170. Sometimes the outdoor jolliness seemed to be a little forced. On this cover of *Health and Life* from 1923, the girls pretend to play in a jazz band at the beach. They "take their deep-breathing exercises" by expanding their lungs, "blowing 'Swanee River' out of their instruments." One suspects that this was just an excuse to show girls in bathing suits on the cover of a magazine.

171. The American magazine *Health and Life* began publication in 1922, and by the time this cover appeared in 1923, a formula had been established. Editor Bernard Bernard regularly presented articles on health, exercise, and sex. He also regularly put pretty girls on the cover. For this issue, strongman, "wrist turner," and wrestler George Jowett posed with "The Pittsburgh Venus."

HOW I LEARNED to LOVE
Health and Life
25 Cents

Spring Number, 1925

"DAINTY MARIE" IN ONE OF HER FAMOUS EXERCISES

I Have Found the Way To Fitness—By Sophie Tucker

THE PSYCHOLOGY OF LOVE   GOOD EXERCISES FOR BABY

WHY SOME MEN AND WOMEN CANNOT LOVE

Health and Life

Edited By Bernard Bernard

20 Cents

JULY, 1923

THE MUSIC OF HEALTH

During a spell in their swimming, these Health and Life Girls take their deep breathing exercise to music, providing their own music, and expanding their lungs in blowing "Swanee River" out of their instruments

A Few of the Brilliant Articles In This Issue Are:

How Athletics Saved My Life
By J. W. Collins

The Romantic Story of Fred Thomson

With the Men of Iron

The Practice of Auto-Suggestion

Tenso-laxing Exercises
By T. J. Allen, M. D., D. O.

Has Your Boy Long Hair?
By the Editor

How I Made Myself 10 Years Younger—By John M. Hernie

How Stecher Does the Scissors Hold

Sunshine—Nature's Vitamine

Is Your Face Your Good Fortune?
By J. Richmond

Sammie and Samson—Funnies

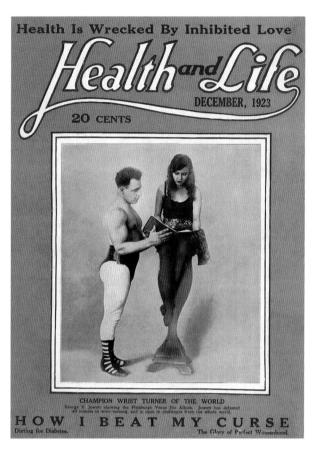

Health Is Wrecked By Inhibited Love

Health and Life

DECEMBER, 1923

20 CENTS

CHAMPION WRIST TURNER OF THE WORLD

George F. Jowett showing the Pittsburgh Venus His Album. Jowett has defeated all comers in wrist-turning, and is open to challenges from the whole world.

HOW I BEAT MY CURSE

Dieting for Diabetes.

The Glory of Perfect Womanhood.

172. Although her professional name was Stanil Lawa, she was actually Mrs Jack Barr of Thibodaux, Louisiana. In her strongwoman act, she broke sixty penny spikes with her teeth, bent an iron bar in her jaw (shown here), and drove nails with her bare hands. This Southern belle was not to be messed with.

173. Stanil Lawa was the highly unusual name of a strongwoman who made the rounds of the few remaining vaudeville theaters in the mid-1930s. She posed for this rare double-biceps photo in 1936, though she doesn't flex her arms as a modern bodybuilder would; she does not clench her hands to full fists. Perhaps she was afraid of showing too much muscle.

174. Strongwomen performed on French street corners in the nineteenth century, but very few of them looked like the woman in these erotic postcards c. 1920. This is part of a series of postcards showing half-naked women posed to look like they are performing various sports. The woman is surrounded by the tools of the traditional strongman's trade—megaphone, drum, weights, and carpet, and she points to her own muscular arm—but even the French (who have a much higher tolerance for public nudity than the Anglo-Saxons) would have objected to this sort of thing.

175. In this postcard, the "strongwoman" does a one-armed press of a fake barbell, but who can look at this photograph without zeroing in on her bare breast and hairy armpit? French sports historian Theirry Terret claims that pictures like this show the degradation of women. I find them oddly charming. *Chacun à son goût.*

To vīru, kas šai nagos kritīs,
Kā spilvenu tā mīcīs, sitīs!

176. The bare-breasted "lady Hercules" pretends to press a barbell, but the whole scene is faked. Athletes like this one existed only in the naughty postcards or fevered imaginations of certain men. If any strongwoman had actually appeared on a Parisian street in this attire, she would have been very popular (but quickly arrested).

177. This comic postcard from Riga, Latvia, was mailed in 1929, but its worried message about women's strength is current. A free translation of the inscription is: "I am waiting to see if what she grabs in her hands is what she will later beat like a pillow!"

178. Although she is a bit too hefty for modern tastes, this vaudeville artist known only as Lundini was apparently very proud of her muscular body. One can assume that she was an escape artist because the words *Wer fesselt mich* ("Who will tie me up?") are written in the lower right. Either that or she was into some extremely kinky stuff.

179. Perhaps this weightlifting beauty was some long-forgotten movie starlet, but if so, no identification has survived. That fact that she is raising a rather large dumbbell is an indication that she is some sort of fitness model. The ribbon around her calf is a charming if mysterious addition to her outfit.

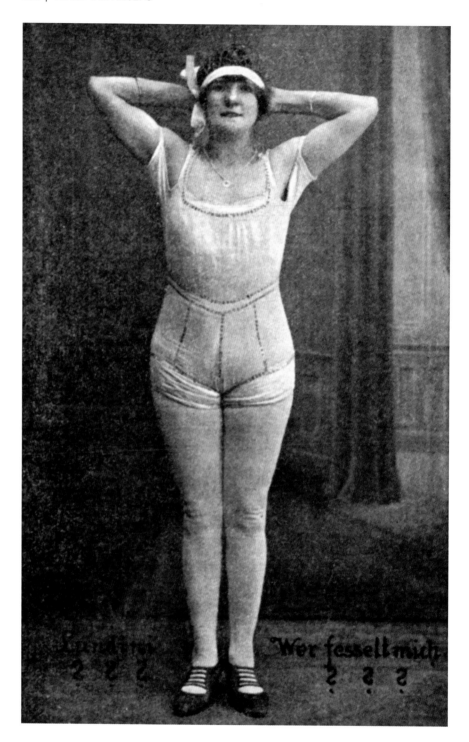

180. In the 1920s and '30s, many Germans were fascinated with the *Lebensreform Bewegung* (Life Reform Movement), an attempt to make life healthier, happier, and more productive through exercise, living closer to nature, and nudism. Gerhard Riebicke took this photo in 1926, and it supposedly demonstrates that grace and beauty could be attained by romping about naked outdoors. Hitler put an end to such notions when he came to power, but later allowed naturism, seeing it as a way to improve Aryan racial stock.

181. Exercising outdoors became a popular activity during the inter-war period. Such tenets of the Life Reform Movement began in Germany, but soon spread to other countries and cultures. Air baths and other forms of cavorting in the open air became huge fads; parasols were out and sunbathing was in. These English girls from the early 1930s seem to be enjoying themselves as they dance by a river.

182. Germany's Life Reform Movement was echoed in many places around the world in the years between the two world wars, as shown on this daring magazine cover from Australia. Topless cover girls are generally considered a modern phenomenon. Not so, as we see on this issue of *Health and Physical Culture*.

183. Women's physical culture flourished even in the Caribbean. Here is a very rare issue of a magazine published in Havana in 1929. The cover illustration shows gymnastics instructor Señora Maucha Marquez de Ferreira and a group of her well-heeled pupils. They could all be found at the Hébert Gymnasium, described as "a great center of women's physical culture worthy of our capital, and where daily they converge to beautify and to strengthen a chosen group of ladies from our best society."

Cultura Física
y Mental
SALUD, FUERZA Y BELLEZA

Organo Oficial del Instituto Nacional de Educación Física

SRA. MAUCHA MARQUEZ DE FERREIRA
Profesora de Cultura Física, y un grupo de sus alumnas.

PRECIO: 20 CTS.   HABANA   ENERO DE 1929

184. Glamorous women exercised to control their weight, firm up their figures, and stay healthy. By the mid-1930s even movie sex-goddess Mae West was proud to be photographed working out with a tiny dumbbell in her boudoir while wearing a skimpy costume.

185. Hollywood starlets always seem to demonstrate exercise equipment that they clearly do not need. This platinum-haired beauty from the mid-1930s uses a home exercise device that was supposed to make sit-ups more difficult and hence more effective. It appears to modern eyes as if it were invented by a chiropractor who wanted to drum up some business.

186. Both modern science and unscrupulous charlatans came up with ingenious apparatuses that would work off unwanted flab. The challenge was figuring out which gizmo worked and which didn't. In this photograph, we see a rowing machine, wall exerciser, and vaulting horse (they all worked); there is also a hip vibrator and a "mechanical horse" (they didn't). This photograph from the mid-1930s may be a production still from a motion picture.

187. Like those of other nations, Italian women wanted to have slender, youthful bodies. There was a long history of women's exercise in Italy; it was one of the first countries in nineteenth-century Europe to require female gymnastics in state schools, and it remained in the forefront of innovative physical exercise. When the Fascists gained power in the mid-1920s, the importance of having strong, healthy mothers to bear and raise good solders became all the more important. Books like *Cultura fisica della donna* (*Women's Physical Culture*) appeared in 1932, encouraging women to exercise.

188. Malaya's only physical culture magazine, *Modern Physical Cult*, was one of the far-flung results of a growing interest in female exercise that began in the 1930s. This issue from 1933 features a pretty Eurasian girl posed pertly in a slightly Art Deco design frame. Her trim figure, stylish bathing suit, and sporting stance show that women's exercise and fitness was truly an international phenomenon.

189. Madame Irène Popard was a professor of female physical education in Paris who produced this little booklet c. 1930 for women who wanted to improve their health and poise by the use of "harmonious gymnastics," which consisted principally of dance and flexibility moves. Women who purchased this little opus hoping to find tips on weightlifting or strength building would be sadly disappointed.

190. Richard Kline, the exercise instructor at Paramount Studios, specialized in training Hollywood stars to become "lovely, graceful, charming, radiantly healthy." This booklet from 1937 featured calisthenics and stretching movements demonstrated by such screen beauties as Ida Lupino (on the cover) and Dorothy Lamour.

191. Ivy Russell was born in Surrey, England, in 1907. Starting in the early 1930s, she was recognized as one of the most powerfully built women who had ever lived. Thanks to her remarkable strength and muscularity, she was successful at wrestling, lifting weights, and displaying her physique. She is shown here at the age of twenty-six. Russell's lean and sinewy body was extremely unusual for a woman at the time, as was her willingness to be photographed in such an aggressive pose. In 1937, it was reported that her biceps were exactly the same size as those of German heavyweight boxer Max Schmeling. It is unclear if this comparison was complimentary to either athlete.

192. Ivy Russell was one of the first modern female bodybuilders in history. According to strength historian Jan Todd, "Russell was a new archetype for women weightlifters [...] her achievements served to convince many other women, both in Great Britain and the United States, that strength and womanhood were not incompatible and that weightlifting was compatible with athletics." Her completely unprecedented physical appearance was quite a change from the more "fleshly" ideals of previous centuries. Here was a woman who was strong, athletic, and unrepentantly muscular—and the world had never seen anything quite like her before.

193. Scottish photographer Ron Rennie took this famous picture of Ivy Russell in 1932. Her sinewy physique and pronounced musculature are apparent in this and the previous two pictures.

194. Although Bernarr Macfadden's flagship magazine *Physical Culture* was the first to devote itself to exercise and fitness, by the 1930s it had gradually morphed into a women's magazine. This issue from June 1939 features the results of a thirty-day reducing diet, and its cover displays the transformation of an overweight matron into a slim and beautiful girl. While Europe was preparing for war, America's women were blithely worrying about the size of their hips.

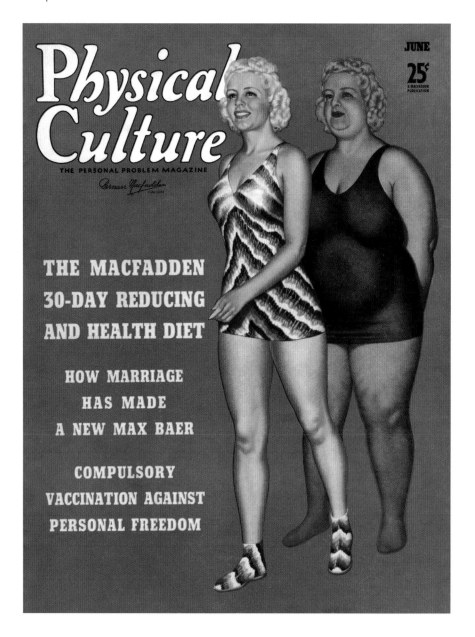

WONDER WOMEN

Strong, forceful females were destined to come to the forefront once more, and the agent of that change was another global conflict. Women had played a relatively minor role in the war effort during World War I; a few took over men's jobs and acted as nurses or ambulance drivers, but there was no real place for females in the allied armies. All that changed during the second great war of the century. The Women's Army Corps was organized in 1942 in the United States, and in that same year a new comic book, *Wonder Woman*, hit American newsstands featuring a strong, intelligent, confident Amazon who did not need a man to do her fighting. Comic book readers in Great Britain had seen the debut of *Sheena, Queen of the Jungle* in 1937, the first comic devoted entirely to a heroic female, but most British and European comics featuring strong women soon disappeared—done in either by wartime paper shortages or Nazi censors. Fortunately, both *Wonder Woman* and the new military units for females thrived in North America (the Canadian Women's Army Corps, or CWAC, was formed in 1941) where they provided girls and women with new models of strength and self-reliance. Careers in the armed forces, professional sports, and in defense factories were now open to girls with grit and gumption. This newly found power was reflected in women like Abbye "Pudgy" Stockton, who advocated weight training for women in her widely respected magazine column, "Barbelles," which first appeared in *Strength and Health* in 1944 and continued for nearly a decade. Girls were not expected to pack on muscles, but many wanted to stay tough enough to do the work now being demanded of them and shapely enough to stay attractive to their soldier boyfriends. Even the pinups of the era began to show women working out. Weight training could be very sexy.

The war years provided plenty of role models if a girl wanted to be forceful, assured, and athletic. These included a semi-fictional war industry worker in Canada known as "Ronnie, the Bren Gun [a type of machine gun] girl," but the most famous of these female defense plant employees was Rosie the Riveter, an imaginary personification of real-life working women in America's war effort. Rosie was made famous in a popular song by bandleader Kay Kyser and an even more popular 1943 *Saturday Evening Post* cover by Norman Rockwell. Thanks to these symbols of female empowerment, thousands of women became accustomed to their new roles in wartime society.

Women were expected to take over for the menfolk while they were away fighting foreign oppressors. Even so, there was plenty of homegrown oppression if one looked closely enough. A confident, self-reliant woman was seen as a threat to many men, and nowhere was this more evident than in such all-male preserves as barbers' waiting rooms, auto repair shops, and gymnasiums. In 1941, Siegmund Klein, proprietor of the most famous bodybuilding gym in North America, fumed about the women who wanted to lift weights. They were not welcome in his establishment, reported an article in the New York tabloid *PM Weekly*. Klein would later change his tune when it became clear that the girls (potential paying customers, after all) were not going to go away. He was not the only man in the 1940s who had to get used to the idea of women who wanted to muscle their way into the old boys' club of strength and athletics.

After World War II, most men expected women to return to their former lives of domestic chores and respectful submission to the male will. Some women shared this expectation, but not all. The immediate postwar years saw a gradual decrease in magazine and newspaper coverage of muscular women. In the middle decades of the twentieth century, powerful girls were treated more as curiosities and objects of ridicule than as role models or elite athletes.

There was a brief period of afterglow for Anglo-American female athletes in the late 1940s. During that time, women like Relna Brewer, Pudgy Stockton, Dorcas Lehman, and other athletes were respected for their physiques and recognized as bona fide athletic stars. They were valued as the same sort of women who helped win the war, whether as members of the armed forces or as defense workers. But in the postwar period, many women set aside their welding torches, uniforms, and weights, and returned to traditional house roles as wives and mothers. Rosie the Riveter was replaced by Lucy Ricardo. Women would have to wait thirty years before being strong and muscular was acceptable again.

195. Women weightlifters were enough of an anomaly in 1942 that Gordon Venables, author of the "Incredible but True" column in *Strength and Health* magazine, featured Evelyn Smith's impressive lift. The illustration that he created for the article is indicative of the times: Evelyn is shown as a shapely pinup, with skimpy costume, perky breasts, and high heels.

196. Nina Unus was only twenty-five years old when she lifted a 150-pound weight overhead with no previous practice or training. This photograph was taken of her c. 1940 when she performed her first feat of strength. To celebrate her newfound strength, young Nina did something very few women did in those days: she flexed her biceps for the camera.

197. *Strength and Health* publisher Bob Hoffman was always stringing along several girlfriends at a time. If they had any talent for strength, exercise, or lifting, he featured them in his magazine. One of the most powerful was Dorcas Lehman. In this photo from 1941, she displays an arm "of which most any bar bell [sic] man would be proud."

198. According to Hoffman, many of his readers preferred "a girl who has strength and muscle" to the slender "undeveloped" beauty-pageant type. Large and lovely Dorcas Lehman fit the bill admirably. She is shown here in 1941.

199. Dorcas Lehman clowns around in this photo by lifting to arm's length a "l00 pound Victory Bar bell [sic]." She is not performing a sanctioned lift, but she does succeed in getting the thing aloft. This photo was taken in 1942, and iron weights would soon be hard to find when wartime restrictions kicked in.

200. Illustrator Gordon Venables was presumably attempting to show that strong women are sexy women. His full-page illustrations displaying "five body-beautifying exercises for the ladies" are found in the March 1941 issue of *Strength and Health*. The drawings show women working out with small dumbbells and on inclines, but—in keeping with the tenor of the times—they also wear bikini halter-tops and high heels.

201. Sexy pictures of women exercising have long been popular subjects of cheesecake illustrators. This artwork from 1940s Italy uses the excuse of a workout to show a scantily clad woman lifting a pathetically small barbell with weights, Indian clubs, and a jump rope at her feet. The fallen strap of her negligee, however, reveals the real reason for this image.

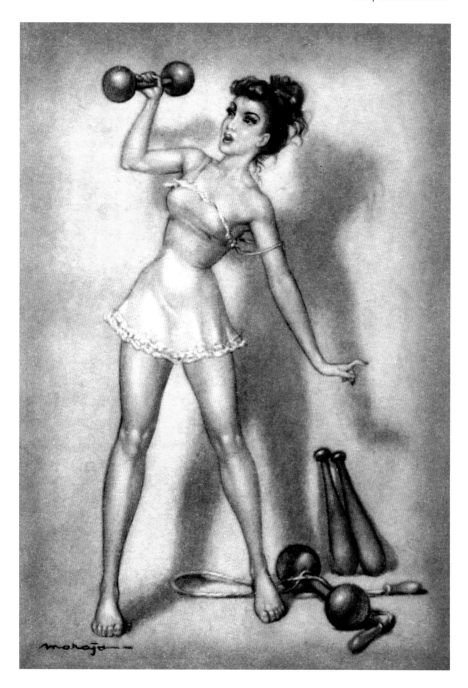

202. In the 1940s, many people still thought it was "unladylike" for girls to handle weights or show their physical prowess. Gracie Bard apparently did not hold that view. Here she cavorts on a Maryland beach in 1941 with several other hulking athletes, among them two Mr Americas (John Grimek, right, and Steve Stanko, left). Women would soon need the kind of strength and endurance that weightlifting could offer for the upcoming war effort.

203. There were few female athletes as strong or as muscular as Evalynne Smith. "Her biceps are large and hard as nails," confirmed one magazine report. She was also quite a pistol. Figuring that what's sauce for the goose is also delicious for the gander, in 1942 (the same year this photo was taken) she organized a "Mr Fuselage Assembly" beauty contest for male co-workers at the factory where she worked.

204. Evalynne Smith of Santa Monica, California, was strong in every sense of the term. She lifted weights, did acrobatics, performed stunts for the movies, was a champion diver and a talented wrestler. And that was just in her spare time. She was a real-life Rosie the Riveter, working in a defense plant when she was not engaged in her strenuous hobbies and recreations. This photo was taken in 1942.

205. Loretta Zygowicz of Chicago was convinced that she could become the strongest woman in the world. It was said that she tossed her 220-pound brother around with ease. This photograph taken c. 1940 by an unknown cameraman is a minor masterpiece; the low camera angle and the lines of the posing costume all help to emphasize her powerful upper body.

206. Six years made a great deal of difference in Loretta's development. By the time this photo was taken in 1946 she had added bulk and muscle due to her use of heavy weights. This is exactly the kind of body that many people feared would result from women's weight training: heavy, graceless, and extremely strong. By this time, Loretta had changed her mind about becoming the world's strongest woman—she wanted to become the world-champion woman wrestler.

207. Jean Ansorge was the wife of a well-known gym owner, but according to this entry from the "Incredible but True" column in *Strength and Health* (December 1941), she was pretty strong in her own right. She is shown here in the midst of her clean and jerk lift.

208. An English nurse named Gladys Waters wrote to an American friend, Angelo Hall, in May of 1942. Since both she and her correspondent were interested in weight training and working out, she sent him a number of photos of herself. In this first group, Gladys exercises outdoors in her bra and knickers. In her letter she admits that she loves lifting, and it is clear from her pictures that she is neither a prude nor a weakling.

209. In the second group of photos, Gladys Waters is more daring. It appears that Miss Waters was not your average reserved English girl. She has a beautiful shape and knows how to display it well. Her youthful beauty and high spirits are made all the more poignant because, just a few months after she sent her American pen-pal these photos, she was shipped off to war. In December of 1942, she was killed at sea during the invasion of Italy when her transport ship was sunk.

210. The publisher of *Strength and Health* magazine, Bob Hoffman, generally liked his women full-figured and strong, and he featured a number of these powerful, unsophisticated girls in the pages of his magazine. In the early 1940s, he was interested in Alda Ketterman; this very flattering drawing of her appeared in 1943.

211. Populations of male war workers in urban areas increased during the war, and their need for unsophisticated after-work diversions were catered to by savvy promoters. Professional wrestling was one sport that saw a great upsurge in popularity during in the 1940s. Soon women were attracted to the sport; one of the first was Gladys "Killem" Gillem. She is shown here in a particularly menacing pose from 1941. The article accompanying the photo takes pains to point out that Gladys is "just as feminine, just as home loving, just as interested in clothes, beauty methods and other similar interests so dear to the heart of most women."

212. By 1942, the United States was at war with the Axis, and girls wanted a superheroine to call their own. *Wonder Woman* was first published in that initial year of America's war effort, an instant hit with both boys and girls. The mighty Amazon warrior led American soldiers in their fight against the Nazis on the cover of the comic book. Wonder Woman did a lot of things that demure little girls were not supposed to do: use aggressive physical strength, insert herself into dangerous situations, and take no guff from men.

213. Before *Wonder Woman*, there was only one comic book dedicated to the exploits of a mighty female character. *Sheena, the Jungle Queen* first appeared in Great Britain in 1937 and a year later in the United States. By November 1942, when this issue of *Jumbo Comics* appeared, she had become an established character in the comic book pantheon. In an unusual reversal of roles, she rescues a helpless man as he is about to be devoured by a wild beast.

214–16. A whole other world of freedom, physicality, and empowerment opened up for women in the 1940s. In addition to participating in sports and working in defense plants, they could also join the military. The Women's Army Corps was formed shortly after the declaration of war in 1942 with the original intention of freeing up men for fighting. A new aggressive spirit soon found its way into the WACs, as these contemporary postcards attest. Lest military male egos feel threatened, the cartoonist muted his positive portrait of army women by having his female soldier use a rolling pin to "WAC" Hitler and by showing a leering man peeping up the skirt of the female paratrooper. Despite the sexism, army life still gave women a new power, attractiveness, and confidence.

217. The Army was not the only branch of the service that saw the advantages of enrolling women. This ad for Camel cigarettes from 1943 shows women in all branches of the service (and all puffing merrily away on Camels). Women had to endure similar physical training regimens as their male counterparts, so these girls are fit. They would need that physical endurance for their new war work—and to protect their "T-zones."

218. When the United States finally entered the war late in 1942, it quickly became clear that women would be needed to fill in for the men who were off fighting in Europe and the Pacific. Artist Vernon Grant created this poster for the war effort in 1944. It shows women working at tasks that required both strength and stamina, and no one wondered if they could handle the job.

"Good Work, Sister
WE NEVER FIGURED
YOU COULD DO A
MAN-SIZE JOB!"

America's Women
HAVE MET THE TEST!

219. Jack Campbell designed this strong depiction of a scowling woman who directs all her rage into her gun-like drill aimed straight at the country's enemies. This image, c. 1943, is not one of friendly cooperation, but rather emphasizes the substantial and serious contributions of women and their part in the conflict. Her somewhat angry comment also illustrates the demand by many females to be valued for their contributions to the war effort by a male-dominated society. Gender roles were changing rapidly, and this woman is clearly not going to be shunted aside just because of her sex.

220. Although to modern viewers it seems to drip with condescension, this poster probably represents the feelings of many male workers during the war. The grudging respect that the woman receives from her manly co-worker was clearly meant to be complimentary, but it's a good thing the man did not say the same thing to the woman in the previous poster. (He might have been drilled where he sat.) The artist Packer created this work in 1944.

221. The decade of the 1940s was largely wracked by the scourge of war and its aftermath, but for North American women it was a time of tremendous physical awakening. Girls discovered that they could do many things that had previously been forbidden to them. Playing professional sports was certainly in this category. In 1943, baseball owners realized that their star players were all being drafted, so they came up with a novel solution, the All-American Girls Professional Ball League (AAGPBL). Here, Pauline "Hedy" Crawley catches a fly ball as she plays for the Peoria Redwings sometime between 1946 and 1951.

222. The AAGPBL was characterized by an extraordinary skill level, high attendance records, and impractical uniforms. Inez "Lefty" Voyce of the Grand Rapids Chicks gets ready to belt the ball. Male audiences were treated to just enough skin to make things interesting, but the short skirts meant that sliding was a painful prospect. Girls' pro baseball ended in 1954 when attendance at the men's games got back up to speed after the war.

Dear Mr. Hoffman:

I've read a good many issues of S.&H. and noted in your Readers' column that several wish the girls left out of the magazine. I for one thoroughly agree with it. The women have several nationwide magazines, have access to all the weeklies and the like, and "Esquire" is the first magazine that they pick up in a doctor's office. I know the world is going to the women but, for God's sake, let's keep one magazine for the men.

I don't begrudge women from weightlifting, in fact I think it's a good idea. If they must have a magazine, give them one. Call it Health and Strength or something like that. They will never be satisfied until you do. However please, I pray to you, keep them out of S.&H. The magazine is tops. The only one I read every article in, of all those I glance at, and I say keep up the good work. Don't let the men down. Please!

Yours truly,

Harold Miller.

223. The greatest of the female pro wrestlers from the mid-1930s to the early 1950s was a muscular dynamo named Mildred Burke. The matches might have been fakes, but Mildred's muscles and athletic talent were real. As one critic remarked, "Wrestling her was a rotten way to make a living." Trying to be an independent female athlete in a man's sport was equally rotten, and Burke (whose real name was Mildred Bliss) took her share of lumps before establishing the World Women's Wrestling Association in the early 1950s to promote her sport.

224. Some men were clearly uncomfortable with strong women, as this letter to the editor of *Strength and Health* from August 1944 attests. Other letters were even more strident. "I like my women feminine," writes one angry man earlier in 1944, "and I cannot see anything feminine about a mannish dressed, cigarette-smoking, beer-guzzling woman … When women begin to compete with men in men's own fields of strength, skill, etc., then to me they cease to be feminine and become sexless."

225. Here is Edna Rivers, just the sort of uppity girl that many men were worried about in 1944. She does a massive 505-pound dead lift. Pudgy Stockton writes about her in the very first column of "Barbelles"; Pudgy is quick to point out that Edna might be powerful, but she is entirely feminine when she is not at the gym. Many women (and a great many men) were not entirely convinced.

226. The unknown subject of this photograph is almost certainly a lady wrestler. Women had been wrestling one another professionally since 1937, but the decade of the 1950s was the golden age of wrestling for both men and women. Stars like Mildred Burke and the "Fabulous Moolah" (Mary Lillian Ellison) made the distaff side of the sport nearly as popular as their male counterparts.

227. A glamorous pose, a possibility of violence and a touch of savagery: these were all the hallmarks of the female wrestler known as The Fabulous Moolah. She was born in rural South Carolina in 1923, but Moolah sometimes claimed that she was from South Africa and had inherited the ferocity of a lioness. In the rockem-sockem world of women's pro wrestling, Moolah was a woman of many talents; she used her skills as a fighter, promoter, and instructor to stay at the top of a very raucous heap. This photo taken c. 1955 displays her exotic beauty to good effect.

228. Gloria Barattini was a shapely farm girl from near Knoxville, Tennessee, who started wrestling in the 1950s. She studied music and was planning on becoming an opera singer, but wrestling won out. She was reportedly a ferocious adversary in the ring.

229. The syndicated comic strip *Ella Cinders* began in 1925 and continued for over fifty years. As the stepdaughter of Myrtle "Ma" Cinders, Ella did the household chores, though she was helped by others, including her boyfriend Waite Lifter. In these two strips from 1946, Ma has decided to become a lady wrestler. Both women's pro wrestling as well as weight training for females come in for a good degree of ridicule in the story.

230 (*above*). One woman more than any other changed our concept of what a fit woman looked like; she was a California girl named Abbye Eville. In the late 1930s, she began lifting the weights her boyfriend had given her in order to improve her chubby physique. It was because of her plump build that she had acquired the nickname "Pudgy," but as her fat dropped away and her muscles began to appear, that name became an ironic testament to what she used to be. In this photo (taken by Cecil Charles, c. 1945), Pudgy shows what a woman can look like if she trains with weights.

231 (*left*). The boyfriend who gave Pudgy some weights to start with was a young UCLA student named Les Stockton, and the two later married. Les was an accomplished athlete in his own right and would later run a gymnasium in Santa Monica. They were an athletic duo, and enjoyed doing acrobatic stunts on the sands of Muscle Beach. Because women took on many tradition-ally male tasks during the war, it was not surprising in the 1940s to see women who could lift weights and pal around with the guys.

232. In addition to being a superb athlete, Pudgy Stockton was also an eloquent proponent of women's weight training. In 1944, she began her regular column in *Strength and Health* magazine, "Barbelles," showing women that they could lift weights and still retain their feminine beauty and charm.

233. Ripping a large telephone book in two was a favorite stunt of many strongmen, and in this sequence, Relna McRae does the honors for the Los Angeles directory of 1944. This feat requires great arm and hand strength, and Relna clearly had both.

234. Relna McRae was almost as famous as Pudgy Stockton, and her weight-trained physique glowed with the same intense healthiness as her more famous friend. Relna was a familiar performer on Muscle Beach, a Southern California venue that was fast becoming a mecca for bodybuilders of both sexes. Here, McRae supports a totem pole of three other people whose combined weight was reported to be 325 lbs.

235. This anonymous woman was probably an acrobat, strongwoman, or trapeze artist in an English circus, and in this photo she works out with a block weight. Circus folk had long known that weightlifting was the best way to maintain one's strength. This picture dates from the late 1940s or early '50s.

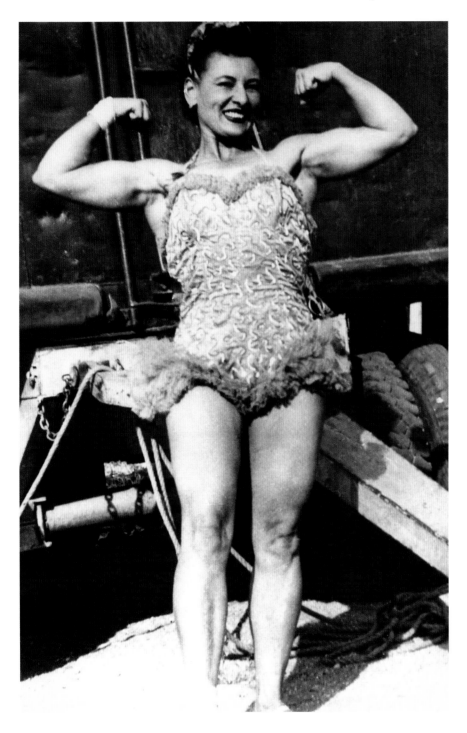

236. In the 1940s and '50s, there were few places where muscular women congregated; one of the most important was in the circus. Aerialists, trapeze artists, and acrobats all developed impressive musculature by practicing their arts. There was a cadre of men who pursued these women and captured their flexing biceps on film. The pictures do not show much creativity or talent, but they document female muscularity at a time when such images were very rare. There is a rustic charm to these photographs, taken in off-hours in front of circus wagons or company busses. Unfortunately, few paying customers wanted to see girls posing like this.

237. This cheerful circus performer seems proud of her upper body as she flexes her arms. Her glamorous, frilly costume contrasts with her bulging muscles and the rough, workaday background of the circus wagon. Photos like these were sold via mail order, and interested men could purchase them easily. What they did with them is anybody's guess.

238. A European athlete does a side press with a block weight in this photo from the late 1940s. Women's interest in weight training was becoming an international phenomenon.

239. Pudgy Stockton was an inspiration to many women. Around 1948, Cecil Charles took this photograph of a few of the women who were encouraged by Pudgy. Relna Brewer McRae (far left) became well-known among the muscular women of Muscle Beach in the 1940s and '50s.

240. In February 1947, the first women's weightlifting meet was held in Los Angeles. A contest for men had preceded it, and the event was sparsely attended. There were only three weight categories: light, middle, and heavyweight, but no overall winner was declared. In this photo by Cecil Charles, the center contestant is Edna Rivers, who won the heavyweight class; to the right of Edna is Pudgy Stockton (middleweight), and to the right of Pudgy is the lightweight winner, Vera Fried.

241. The year 1947 was notable in the history of bodybuilding, as Steve Reeves brought new glamour to the Mr America contest (which he won that year), and Pudgy Stockton traveled to the East Coast for a series of guest appearances. This program from a strength and variety show in New Haven, Connecticut, was for one of those events. Although there were many famous strongmen and bodybuilders on the bill, Pudgy's portrait was on the cover.

CONNECTICUT

Weight Lifting

Association

ANNUAL

STRENGTH and

VARIETY SHOW

SUNDAY, NOVEMBER 16, 1947.

2 P. M.

SAINT MICHAEL'S HALL

Cor. Chestnut & Green Sts.

NEW HAVEN, CONNECTICUT.

PUDGY STOCKTON

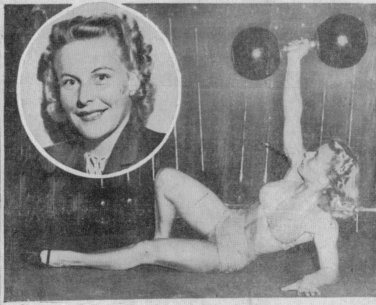

NEW YORK WORLD-TELEGRAM, WEDNESDAY, NOVEMBER 12, 1947

Meet Mr. and Mrs. Muscles

Her nickname is Pudgy, but that's strictly a misnomer for Mrs. Abbye Stockton, as anyone can plainly see, at left, above and at right. For your information, moreover, that's her 182-pound husband, Les, she's toting around, at right.

World-Telegram Photos by Palumbo.

Queen of Bar-Belles, Champ Weight Lifter, Supports Her 182-Pound Husband as Hobby

By MURRAY ROBINSON,
World-Telegram Staff Writer.

wield the bar-bells, a type of weight-lifting apparatus) is Mrs. Abbye Stockton. She is a de-

Jerk. The European weight-lifters in those days had big stomachs. When they lifted a bar-bell, the

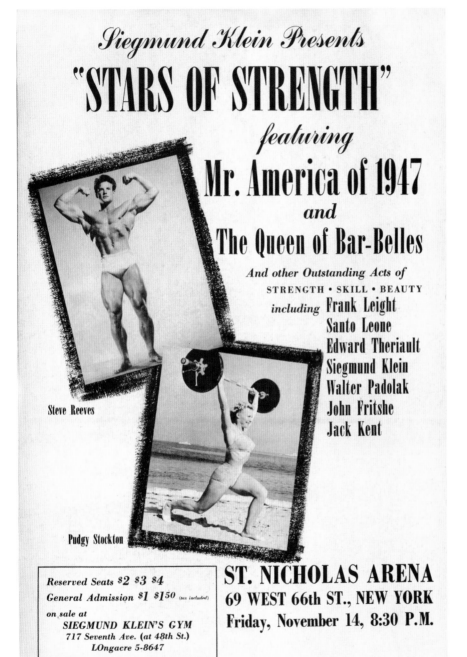

Siegmund Klein Presents

"STARS OF STRENGTH"

featuring

Mr. America of 1947

and

The Queen of Bar-Belles

And other Outstanding Acts of
STRENGTH • SKILL • BEAUTY
including **Frank Leight**
Santo Leone
Edward Theriault
Siegmund Klein
Walter Padolak
John Fritshe
Jack Kent

Steve Reeves

Pudgy Stockton

Reserved Seats *$2 $3 $4*
General Admission *$1 $1*⁵⁰ (tax included)
on sale at
SIEGMUND KLEIN'S GYM
717 Seventh Ave. (at 48th St.)
LOngacre 5-8647

ST. NICHOLAS ARENA
69 WEST 66th ST., NEW YORK
Friday, November 14, 8:30 P.M.

242. Pudgy and her bodybuilder husband Les Stockton became celebrities in a city that was overrun with them. They often received the Hollywood treatment as they walked along the beach. When the two visited New York City, newspapers enjoyed emphasizing the "strongwoman" aspect of their relationship, and Les was usually content to play along with the foolishness. In this 1947 article from the *New York World-Telegram*, the "Queen of the Bar-Belles" indulges in some muscular cheesecake posing.

243. The culmination of their 1947 visit to New York came when Pudgy and the new Mr America, Steve Reeves, appeared in the "Stars of Strength" show at St Nicholas Arena. "Strength • skill • beauty"—Pudgy had them all. She also was a pioneering spirit who brought weightlifting into the lives of hundreds of men and women.

244. The summer of 1947 also saw, on the sands of Santa Monica, California, the first contest independent of the usual weightlifting competitions. More than thirty contestants competed in the Miss Muscle Beach beauty pageant, and virtually none of them had any muscles to speak of. The American public was more interested in seeing pretty girls with slender figures and curves in all the right places.

245. The three top-place winners in the Muscle Beach beauty pageant were (left to right) Val Njord (second place), Vivian Crocket (first place), and Jackie McCullah (third place). Of the three, only Jackie McCullah had actually trained with weights. None of the judges seemed either to notice or mind.

246. The winner of the 1947 Miss Muscle Beach contest, Vivian Crocket, poses here; she was a fit but hardly muscular choice.

247. This cover of muscle magazine *Your Physique* from March 1950 shows popular fitness girl (and runner-up in the 1947 Miss Muscle Beach pageant) Val Njord with shirtless actor Lex Barker, who took over the Tarzan franchise from 1949 to 1953.

248. Model and fitness star Val Njord was promoted in several of publisher Joe Weider's magazines as "the bodybuilders' sweetheart." This cover photograph was taken by physique photographer Bruce Bellas in 1949. Njord was a Swedish stenographer who went to California and began modeling in the late 1940s; she achieved her greatest fame in the early 1950s.

249. During the 1940s, movie starlets could be found everywhere in Southern California, and it took very little persuading to get them into bathing suits, parading in front of the public in beauty contests. Although this photo shows the second edition of the "Miss Muscle Beach Contest," there were very few muscles on display—voluptuous glamour was the order of the day, not rock-hard sinews. In this photo, from 1948, the contestants pose on the dais.

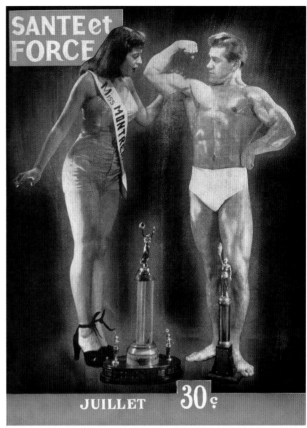

250. This portrait of Réjane Robert by photographer Tony Lanza was published in 1948. The model was the sister of bodybuilder Leo Robert, and she had long trained with light weights and gymnastic exercises. She later became women's editor of *Iron Man* magazine.

251. Miss Montreal for 1948, Kay Parker feels bodybuilder Leo Robert's muscles in this photograph by Tony Lanza. Once again, the woman has been reduced to an amazed admirer of the man. His muscles, not hers, are the main event in this little athletic drama.

252. Marge Eliason poses with her Miss Body Beautiful trophy in 1949. Although she had trained extensively with weights, Mrs Eliason would not have dreamed of showing off any of her muscles. Marge's husband was Alton Eliason, a well-known weight trainer and bodybuilding coach.

253. In this photo from the late 1940s, model "Chicky" Winslow does a few arm curls using tiny, girly weights while her instructor, Siegmund Klein, pumps some serious iron. It is significant that if girls wanted to lift weights, they felt obliged to over-emphasize their femininity; hence the pretty two-piece bathing suit and the high heels (not practical gym gear for serious athletes).

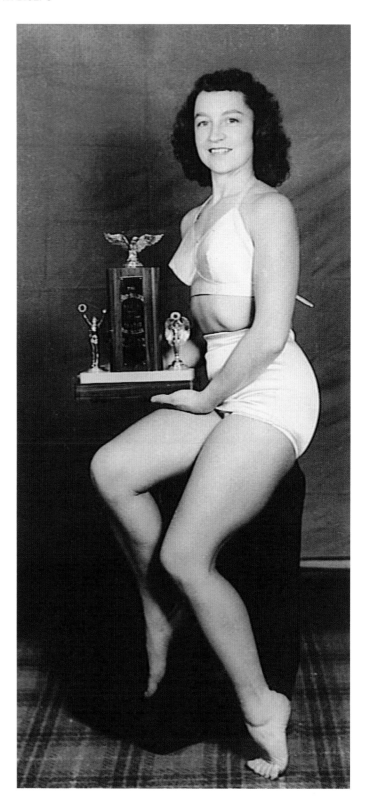

254. Bodybuilding was never easy, but it was even more difficult in postwar Britain with all the problems brought on by an exhausted economy and food rationing. When *Health and Strength* magazine ran their Ladies' Physical Excellence contest in 1946, it was won by Lydia Johnson, the pretty Scottish lass shown on the cover here. The judges thought that she was "a picture of health and vitality." She was not, however, a picture of muscularity—far from it.

255. By 1949, things were improving a bit for women bodybuilders in the UK. This cover photo demonstrates that there was a wider acceptance for physically developed women there, who were given a place on the cover without needing a man to fawn over. Pat Scrivens from Exeter was chosen as Miss South-West Britain, although this issue of *Health and Strength* might merely indicate that the British had discovered (like the North Americans) that photos of bikini-clad girls on the covers helped sell more magazines.

CHAMPION GYMNASTS IN ACTION

JUNE 16th, 1949

SACRED THY BODY
EVEN AS THY SOUL

HEALTH and STRENGTH

6ᴰ

FORTNIGHTLY

The National Physical Fitness Journal

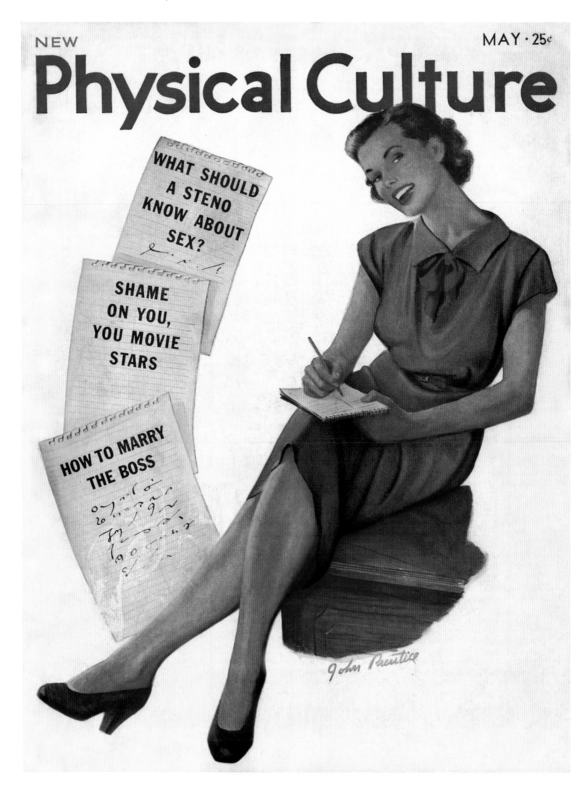

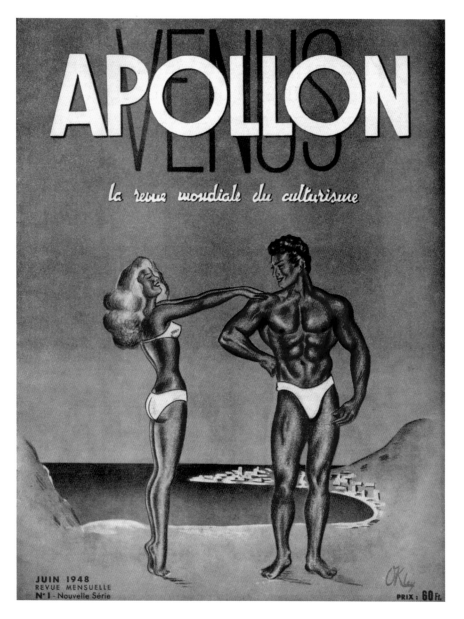

256. The changing times are apparent in *Physical Culture*, Macfadden's once-proud magazine of health and exercise. Even as early as the late 1940s, it had given itself over almost entirely to discussions of sex, marriage, and makeup. This issue contains almost no exercise advice and only a bit about nutrition (mainly reduction diets), and most of the contents focus on how a girl can snag a rich and powerful husband.

257. Marcel Rouet was a French physical culturist and bodybuilder who made a name for himself in the late 1930s. He later parlayed his fame and knowledge into a career as a gym owner and writer of around 100 books on exercise and fitness. In 1948, Rouet started a magazine that catered to both male and female physical culturalists. *Apollon—Venus* did not last long, but it was one of the first periodicals of this type to devote almost half of its pages to women's exercise. This is the cover of the first issue.

258. The delightfully sleazy artwork by O'Klay shows that pioneer though he might have been, Marcel Rouet was not in favor of women's muscularity. The copy promises that Rouet "will make you into a beautiful and seductive woman in three months." This is an ad from 1948 for "the world's first correspondence course in women's physical culture."

259. By 1950, when this issue was published, Wonder Woman had become a pop culture icon. After the end of World War II, she engaged in the struggle against America's new enemies: organized crime, evil geniuses, and the ever-present Red Menace.

(following page)
260. Pudgy Stockton had demonstrated that women could look good and be muscular. Here she poses c. 1954 with her counterpart of male physique beauty, Steve Reeves (who later went on to star in a series of sword-and-sandal movies in the early 1960s). The symbolism of the photo is one of its most interesting elements. It represents male and female athleticism joined by a chaste and muscular handclasp. There is no condescension, no inequality, no implied freakishness. It simply portrays Pudgy's yin to Steve's yang. Unfortunately, much of Pudgy's work was undone in the succeeding two decades as women avoided weights and muscularity and retreated to more traditional and submissive gender roles.

FROM FIGURE TO PHYSIQUE

Something odd happened to strong, muscular women between the 1950s and the mid-1970s. They disappeared. At least they vanished from the public eye; there were no more physical culture contests, no more performing strongwomen, and no more displays of female muscular strength. Women no longer cared to flex their muscles in public—neither physically nor politically—since it was considered by the vast "silent majority" of the time to be bad form (and popular wisdom held that being a strong, opinionated woman was social suicide). Certainly women still appeared on the covers of muscle magazines, but no longer as examples of physical prowess. Now they were simply pretty decorations or admiring dolls who oohed and aahed over the men. Pudgy Stockton's "Barbelles" had been transformed into Eisenhower-era "Dumbbelles." Unfortunately, even many strong women seem to have bought into this metamorphosis.

The men's exercise and bodybuilding magazines continued to feature sections exclusively for women, but these articles emphasized women's beauty, not their strength. Keeping your man happy with a good meal, a clean house, and a shapely figure was more important than building muscles. Even during the otherwise revolutionary 1960s, most women did not consider muscularity a worthy goal, and most men did not consider it a desirable trait in women. It was much more important to have big breasts, a narrow waist, and seductive hips. One historian of women's strength has called the period from 1950 to the late 1970s as the "gestation period" of women's bodybuilding, and it was a long and slow one. It took nearly three decades to coax athletic women back into the gym in order to turn their curves into muscles.

261. By the 1950s, Muscle Beach and its fit and tanned beauties were hitting their stride. In this photograph from the mid-1950s, a crowd of muscle boys hoists up Beverly Jocher. The image evokes the sun, sand, and frenetic activity that could be found almost any day at the popular seaside location.

For over thirty years, strong, muscular women had vanished from magazines, gymnasiums, and public venues. But gradually, women began to realize that suppressing their own strength and individuality was a difficult and largely thankless task. In the 1960s, feminist writers such as Betty Friedan began to reflect the frustration that many women were feeling at being trapped at home. In 1963 she wrote, in *The Feminine Mystique*, of a "strange stirring, a sense of dissatisfaction, a yearning that women suffered in the middle of the twentieth century."

Changes in the gym only slowly reflected the increasing dissatisfaction of women's role in the wider world. Many fit and healthy women were tiring of their roles as simpering sex objects; they wanted to be valued as athletes like the men were. In 1977, the movie *Pumping Iron* was released, and it created a new interest in both the sport of men's competitive bodybuilding and in the film's star, Arnold Schwarzenegger. In that same year, women's involvement in the sport experienced a revolution.

It was 1977 when Henry McGhee, the director of weight training at the YMCA in Canton, Ohio, had the idea of presenting a bodybuilding competition for women that would judge the participants' muscularity, not their poise or beauty. To this end, McGhee established the United States Women's Physique Association (USWPA), and the first contest was held in November of 1977. The winner was a local athlete with the euphonious name of Gina Laspina, who, as historian Steve Wennerstrom declared, "establish[ed] ground zero for the sport." Shortly after this, Doris Barrilleaux began running bodybuilding competitions in Florida, then various other organizations began to see the trend that was rapidly forming and started their own organizations and competitions.

262. Not all the muscular acrobats at Muscle Beach were men—not even all were adults. In this photograph, c. 1955, a child identified on the back only as April reportedly supports 435 lbs. Despite the girl's diminutive size, she can bear such a heavy burden; this is due largely to women's stronger hips and lower body. They can consequently support much greater weights than men. The huge crowd has come to see a free acrobatic show and to ogle the muscular denizens of the beach.

263. A female lifter does a one-handed dumbbell press c. 1950. Even among men, there was apprehension that weight training would make a man "muscle bound." Far more dangerous and offensive in the public mind were women who wanted to lift weights!

Armand Tanny & Evelyn Lovequist
"Mr. & Miss U.S.A." 1950

264. By the early 1950s, female beauty pageants were often attached to bodybuilding shows ("fungus-like" attachments, as one critic described them). In 1950 Armand Tanny won the Mr USA contest in Los Angeles. Here he is accompanied on the dais by Miss USA, Evelyn Lovequist who, though clearly fit and trim, was hardly in the same muscular league. The pairing of bodybuilding and beauty contests was ended when the men objected to the implication that they were just male counterparts of the beauty queens.

265. In most examples of male and female physique photography from the early 1950s, the woman is a pretty but extraneous appendage to the muscular male. In this unusual photo, the anonymous woman stands in the fore, and her male partner mimics her pose.

266. French Canadian athlete Leo Robert graced the cover of *Iron Man* magazine in 1955 accompanied by his sister Réjane. In this photo, there is less obvious focus on the man (though he is still the star, as his upraised arm proclaims) than in, say, Fig. 251].

267. Inside the magazine, there is another full-page spread featuring Réjane, who is now the author of the special women's feature, "Vivacious Womanhood." No weightlifting information is given; this column aimed to make female readers more shapely and beautiful, not more muscular.

Leo Robert "Mr Universe" and his sister Rejane

Vivacious Womanhood

IRON MAN'S SPECIAL DEPARTMENT FOR WOMEN

268–69. An occasional columnist to *Iron Man* magazine was Alyce Yarick. Her husband, Ed, had a famous gym (Yarick's) in Oakland, California, and Alyce had always been interested in women's exercise. With the postwar baby boom in full swing, it was only natural that exercises that could be done safely during pregnancy would interest many women. Here we are shown some workout routines for expecting mothers. Dumbbell presses on an incline board and squats are both demonstrated in these photographs c. 1955.

270 (*right*). "'Muscle Women' Vie in Weight Lifting" reads the headline from the article that this photo, published in Los Angeles in 1950, accompanies. Mrs Gerry Hodsdon of San Diego, California, shown here, is presumably one of the "muscle women" in the headline. The article announces the first female weightlifting meet sanctioned by the Amateur Athletic Union. Getting the AAU to support women's weightlifting was a hurdle overcome only after much work and lobbying from female athletes and their supportive male colleagues.

A Satisfied Customer

Take the weight off your mind . . . call us NOW!

"Write Something Good About America Today"

West Virginia Mine Supply Co.

CLARKSBURG, W. VA. :: Phone MAin 4-7491

Mill, Mine, Railroad and Contractors' Supplies and Equipment

"We Have It—Can Get It—Or It Isn't Made"

271. This anonymous acrobat or strongwoman lifts weights and swings on the rings in a gymnasium some time in the 1950s or early '60s. If the globe barbells are loaded to their maximum, then she is a woman of extraordinary strength and agility. It is not easy to press or curl such weights, and it is difficult to balance a barbell on the soles of one's feet.

272. Female weightlifters occasionally appear in pinup art, but they are all creatures of male fantasy, not female empowerment. Pretty girls showing more skin than they should, approachable beauty, and pouty lips: these were all hallmarks of the pinup artist Gil Elvgren (1914–80). The name of this image from 1959 is "Shaping Up." Here, one of Elvgren's girls attempts to remove a barbell from its shipping container wearing stockings, high heels, panties, and garter belt. Clearly, the "satisfied customer" referenced in the upper caption is the male owner of this calendar.

273–74. Pinup and cheesecake photos had long featured "weight training" as an excuse to photograph women in suggestive poses. These two images from the 1950s show that it was still a popular alibi. It hardly matters that the weights are fake. No one would have looked at them, anyway.

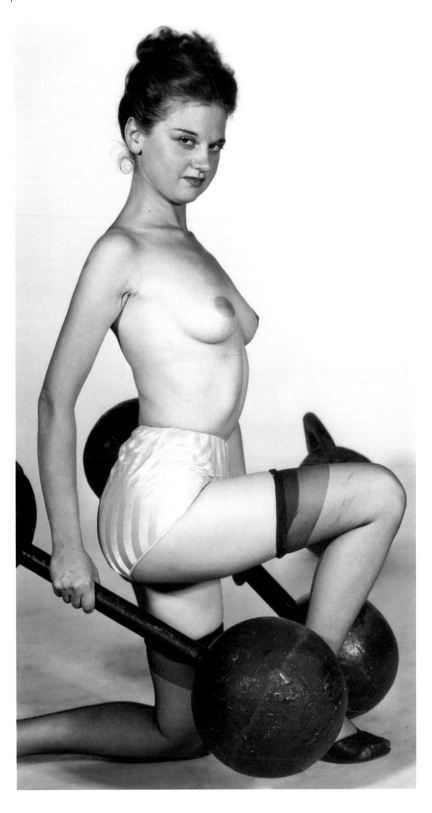

275. France's oldest continuous publication on the subject of health and exercise, *La culture physique*, had long been a supporter of female weight training, but by 1954 (when this issue was published), it was hardly one of their specialties. This cover shows bodybuilder James Mathé "with one of his graceful pupils." Again, the man's muscled abdomen is the most important element in the image: the girl's arm and leg are merely a frame for his midsection.

276. One of the most famous strong-women of the modern era is this beautiful woman, Joan Rhodes, shown here c. 1955. Blessed with movie-star good looks, she established herself as a circus, cabaret, and music hall performer, and was soon traveling all over the world bending iron bars, lifting absurdly heavy weights, and throwing men around like sacks of flour. Her most famous victim in that routine was Bob Hope, whom she regularly toted off the stage at the end of their turn. Was Joan Rhodes (who passed away at the age of eighty-nine on May 30, 2010) really strong, or was she simply a superb performer? The jury is still out.

277. In the 1950s, women were beginning to invade the formerly all-male reserve of the gymnasium, a phenomenon that was noted in the daily comics page. In this episode of *Bringing up Father* from 1952, Jiggs is reconciled to remaining longer at the gym after spying a few of the girls who plan on working out there.

278. Here is another example of a parody from the early 1950s in which the wife, maid, or cleaning woman picks up the man's weights as if they are as light as a feather. There are versions of this hoary joke dating back to the nineteenth century.

"Now please try to be light on your feet, girls, the pool room downstairs always kicks about the noise on Ladies' Day!"

279. Another popular way to poke fun at exercising women is the ridicule them for their weight. Somehow fat women were a lot funnier than over-weight men—at least to the men who drew the comics.

280. By 1963, canons of feminine beauty were changing; thin was in and the voluptuous, Marilyn Monroe look that was so popular a decade earlier was out. *Iron Man*'s women's colum-nist, Réjane Robert, received many letters from her readers complaining that she was too fat, so she went on a "crash program of figure perfection," and this photograph shows the results. As in most fitness photos from that era, the model is dressed and coifed to perfection.

281. *Wonder Woman* was not the only comic book girl to show girls what a strong woman could do. Lois Lane, Superman's sweetheart and a perennial bridesmaid in a world of happily married women, merited her own comic book. In this issue from 1959, Lois's sister Lana acquires super strength. (Fans need not worry; by the final page Lois's heart is mended.)

282. Jack LaLanne was one of the first fitness and exercise gurus to use television to get his message across to the public. *The Jack LaLanne Show* ran for an astounding thirty-four years; the majority of its audience was made up of housewives who were stuck at home but wanted to stay fit. LaLanne recognized who his target audience was almost from the start. He produced this booklet of exercises and diet tips in 1953, six years before his television program was nationally syndicated in 1959.

YOUR FIGURE
BY
Jack LaLanne

PRICE $2.00
(IN U.S.A.)

283. This was an early attempt at a tie-in product. Jack LaLanne's whipped cottage cheese was sold in the San Francisco Bay area in the early 1950s and was one of the items that Jack sold on the air. The fast-talking TV host was always giving nutrition advice, and two classic "LaLanne-isms" include "If man made it, don't eat it," and, "If it tastes good, spit it out."

284. This photo of the entire LaLanne household was part of a Christmas card sent to friends and associates sometime in the early 1960s.

285. LaLanne was a familiar figure on the small screen where he cheerfully led his at-home audience through their callisthenic workouts using only a chair as equipment. He would often look directly at the camera and exhort his female audience to "Get up, work out, and feel better!"

286. Health, beauty, strength, and vigor were the implied qualities bestowed on people who ate A-plus Pears. This was conveyed by the image of a pretty woman athlete on the lithographed box label, c. 1960. The Summer Olympics, held in Rome that year, were another obvious inspiration for the illustration, as indicated by the woman wearing the US national shield on her top.

287. From the mid-1950s to the early 1970s, women had to appear as ladylike as possible, even when doing something as traditionally masculine as working out with weights. This girl is doing a seated press with a respectably heavy weight, but her high heels and helmet-like hairdo are like fig leaves preserving her femininity.

288. Exercising as an erotic act seems to be the real subject of this photograph. Hundreds of images like this were made of girls training with weights and then sold to gentlemen who found such displays enjoyable (which might explain the fetishistic stiletto heels and low-cut top).

289. Yanking on expanders will do your upper body a world of good, but this photograph, c. 1960, seems to emphasize the protruding bosom rather than good strand-pulling technique.

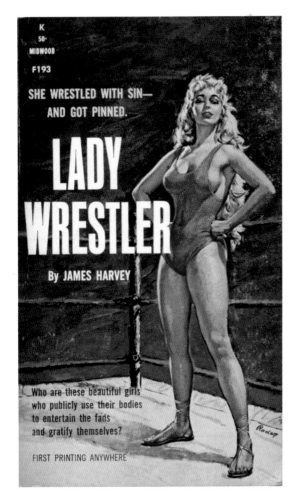

290. Although female wrestlers were almost as formidable as their masculine colleagues, the lady grappler on the cover of this steamy pulp novel, called *Lady Wrestler* (1962), is little more than a sexy caricature of the real thing. "What do these super-gals do for sexual pleasure?" asks the breathless teaser on the back. The blurb then hints at the answer, as it promises to blow the lid off "this grotesque sport where girls pin girls for pay and pleasure." Once again, realities of female strength and muscularity have fallen victim to male fantasies.

291. Even in the mid-1960s, women rarely appeared on the covers of bodybuilding magazines by themselves and never to display their musculature. Here is a typical cover of the time. English model Maureen Gay poses gracefully beside Mr America and Mr Universe winner Joe Abbenda. These two presumably represent the apex of physique beauty for their time. The girl was there to get your attention, but the guy was the real target of visual importance. The implication here is that if you look like the man, you can get the groovy girl. Maureen is presumably putty in the hands of a muscular athlete like Joe.

292. In 1964, the American men's muscle magazine *Strength & Health* began a series called "Miss World Body Beautiful Photo Contest." This was a way to get more pictures of pretty girls into the magazine at no cost whatsoever to the notoriously penny-pinching publisher, Bob Hoffman. The Miss World photos were there to decorate the pages of a man's magazine since there was no connection to female bodybuilding whatsoever. Miss World contestants were a catalog of fit and attractive girls who chose to display their charms for athletic guys. A case in point is Bobbi Vance of Norwalk, Iowa, who balances her impressive rack on the hood of a sports car.

293. Big hair and big breasts were *de rigueur* for contestants in the Miss World Body Beautiful photo competition. Big muscles, not so much. Here, Deborah Cardonick of Philadelphia, Pennsylvania, poses for the camera in 1964.

294. Miss World Body Beautiful contestant Janel Smith of Harrisburg, Pennsylvania, chose to pose in her majorette costume. Although there was some confusion at the time about what a muscular girl should look like, Miss Smith's inclusion in a bodybuilding magazine is clearly for decorative reasons since the photo editors obviously chose her on the basis of her general perkiness and ample proportions. Most of her muscles would seem to be safely out of sight in her baton-twirling wrists.

295. After Pudgy Stockton ended her column "Barbelles" in *Strength and Health* magazine in 1953, another woman came along to demonstrate exercises that were appropriate for women. Vera Christensen (shown here in 1964) began writing articles in 1956, and her monthly column "To the Ladies!" appeared until *Strength and Health* (the word "and" was replaced by an ampersand in the 1960s) ceased publication in 1986. Women in the 1960s and '70s no longer wanted to read advice on weight training, so Christensen's column catered to readers who wanted to look slim and fit, not muscular.

296–97. How things had changed since the 1940s! In 1966, when these photos were taken, women no longer wanted to be strong or muscular; they wanted to look fit and charming—a sexier and slightly more athletic version of 1950s *Leave It To Beaver* übermom June Cleaver. Vera Christensen was perfect for the job of turning her readers into demure housewives with just a little va-va-voom. Here she demonstrates how ordinary household objects familiar to any wife and mother could be used to stay fit. No fancy gym togs? No problem: "I have illustrated these exercises in a skirt, blouse and high heels to show that they can be performed in this sort of garb as well as in a leotard or brief exercise clothes."

298. *Iron Man* columnist Paula
Mollerup wanted to know what female
body shape her readers preferred;
should the ideal be slender and not visibly muscular, or bulging with muscles
like the men? In late 1966, she presented these two drawings, which she had
traced from actual photos, and asked
her readers to decide. Unfortunately,
the promised follow-up article with the
results never appeared.

299. Even the redoubtable Amazon
Wonder Woman had a few personal issues in the mid-1960s. Would she ever
find love or would she spend the rest
of her life in unmarried hell? The un-
spoken message is that the only thing
worse than marrying the wrong man
is not marrying anyone, and women
(even wonder women) need men to
make them truly feminine. In this issue
of the comic book from 1965, Wonder
Woman falls prey to every girl's worst
nightmare: all her friends can see that
her groom is a monster, but she apparently can't. Sometimes even superhe-
roes can screw up their lives.

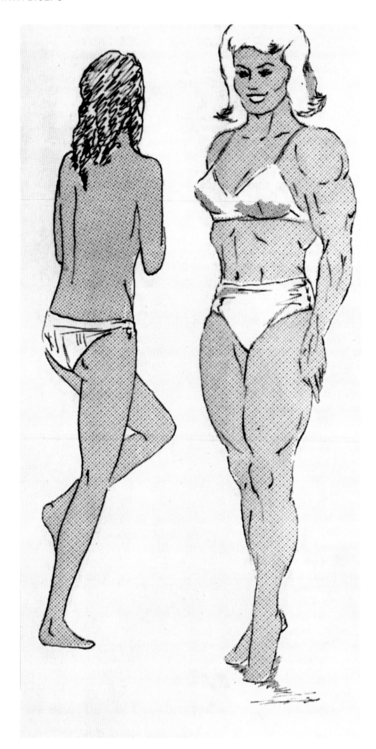

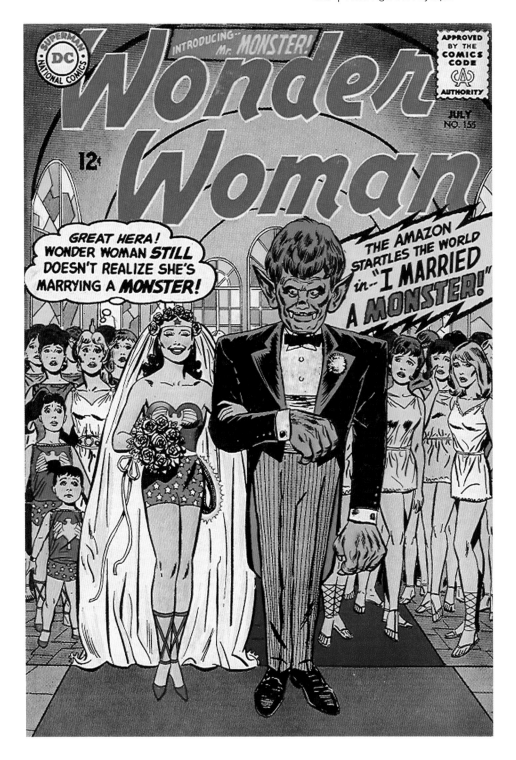

MUSCLES
MAGAZINE
— PARAIT TOUS LES DEUX MOIS —
23ᵉ ANNEE — Nº 146

Votre leçon de culture physique, pour vous, MONSIEUR, et aussi pour vous, MADAME.

EDITE EN BELGIQUE
FRANCE . . 2,90 FRS
BELGIQUE . 29.— FRS
SUISSE . . 2,90 FRS
HOLLANDE . 2,50 Fl.

CONTIENT UNE
PHOTO
GEANTE

Le culturiste français
Christian FERRAND
et sa jolie partenaire
(Photo Luc GESLIN, Paris)

300. In the 1960s, muscular women received little serious and respectful attention from bodybuilders whether they were in Europe or North America. Girls were merely pretty decorations on the cover of most magazines, there to show their admiration or (as in this case) to hang on the man, indicating weakness and dependence. This issue of the Belgian magazine *Muscles* was published in 1968.

301. Readers could occasionally find articles in *Muscles* that were directed toward women. In this article on "The Beauty of Legs," author Georges Dardenne gives about a dozen suggestions for exercises to make women's legs more shapely, only one of which includes working with weights. Lily Plumaans (left) and the author's wife, Monique Dardenne (right), show off their legs in this photo published in 1968.

302. One time-tested way of dealing with muscular women was to ridicule them. This trading card from the popular television program *Rowan & Martin's Laugh-In* pokes fun at both America's enemy in the cold war and Soviet female athletes. The card was issued in 1968.

303. Muscle magazines put women on their covers, but until the end of the 1970s, stuck to the old formula of portraying them as sexy, compliant, and worshipful. In this *Mr. America* cover from 1972, Arnold Schwarzenegger gets his ego stroked from two different directions.

THE MAGAZINE FOR TODAY'S VIRILE MAN ● AUGUST/75c

mr. america

47757 K
25p

WAIST SLIMMING IN A HURRY . . . for that 'sleek look' you've always wanted!
VITAMIN E Can Make You Super Healthy • GAIN UP TO 14 POUNDS IN 14 DAYS . . . and all
solid muscle! • $15 COMPLETE SHAPE-UP COURSE . . . for that really *great* look!
MUSCLE MEN . . . ARE THEY A SEX SUPERMARKET? • NOW . . . 'MEDITATION'
Revolt Of The Masses? • SHAPE-UP YOUR PHYSICAL ECOLOGY
NEW! THE SNACK DIET . . . that performs slimming miracles!

**FOODS THAT GIVE FORCE
TO YOUR SEX LIFE**
'Tis the season to be sensual!

304. In 1974, men had Mr Universe and a number of other important contests, and the women of Britain had "Miss Bikini." When this trio of contestants won, the degrading name of the competition and the skimpy costumes, seductive poses, and voluptuous figures all show that this was little more than a beauty contest, not a bodybuilding one.

305. One of the greatest female athletes of all times, Billie Jean King is shown here appraising Bobby Riggs' arm muscles. In 1973, Riggs (a self-confessed male chauvinist pig) claimed that females did not have the same competitive spirit as men, and he challenged King to a tennis match. Billie Jean won handily in three sets. King was certainly not muscular in the usual sense, but she was superbly athletic and (just as important) unwilling to let women be publicly denigrated.

306. Tigra the Werewoman was a female superhero who appeared in the mid-1970s. Her muscularity, athletic ability, and the superpowers granted to her by a race of cat people made Tigra a fictional embodiment of the raw female power that was starting to be found in both comic books and (in somewhat tamer form) the sporting world.

307. Over three decades after Wonder Woman and Sheena, the world was presented with another powerful female comic book character, Ms Marvel. Despite her striking resemblance to 1970s pinup Farrah Fawcett, Ms Marvel was the first super-heroine to use the newly coined title of Ms. "At last!" reads an excited announcement on the cover, "A bold, new super-hero-ine in the senses-stunning tradition of Spider-Man!" This issue is the first of Ms Marvel's own magazine, released in January of 1977. Ms M. has continued her "senses-stunning" run up to the present.

308. Not surprisingly, Carol Danvers (Ms Marvel's alter ego), works for a feminist magazine called *Woman*. This was clearly based on the real-life *Ms. Magazine*, which was founded in the early 1970s. The comic book thus conflates physical strength and hero-ism with political and social power. Unfortunately, though Ms Marvel's physique is fit (and decidedly buxom), it is not the body of a real physique athlete.

309. One of the few places one could see strong, healthy girls displaying their aggression and athleticism was on the movie screen. Naturally, the fights and hair-pulling were all faked, but no one really cared, least of all the heavy-breathing audiences. This example of an exploitation film, whose title can be translated as *The Bare-Breasted Warrior Women*, was released in 1973. It concerns a group of Amazons who choose a queen by means of a shirtless, girl-on-girl fight, after which the tribe decides to mate *en masse* with Greek warriors. The women are putatively in control in this film, but they are clearly playing to male fantasies.

310. In the 1960s, film directors found that movies featuring hunky gladiators made money, and they soon discovered that films featuring melon-breasted female fighters could also be profitable. These may not have been genuine female athletes, but they were as close as many people in the 1960s and '70s had seen. That was good enough for sleazemeister Roger Corman, who gave the world *The Revolt of the Women Gladiators* (known in English as *Naked Warriors*), produced in 1974. Pam Grier was in this wonderful turkey; she would later achieve greater fame in blaxploitation films as the feisty character Foxy Brown.

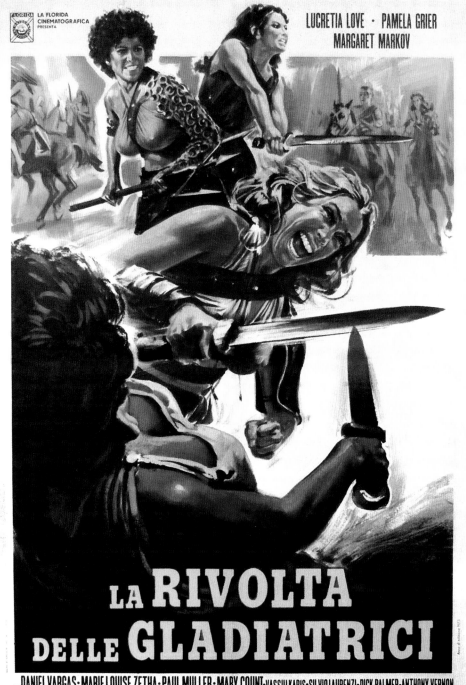

311. One of the most colorful and interesting figures in the early history of women's bodybuilding is Kelli Everts, who not only claimed to be "the progenitor and foundress of female bodybuilding" but also "the stripper for God." She was photographed (with her trophies) for *Esquire* magazine in 1975. Although she had a fit and buxom appearance, Everts does not possess the kind of muscularity that one would expect from a bona fide bodybuilder, how did she win all those awards— were they for beauty, physique, public speaking …? What separated Everts from other women of the time was that she attributed her physique primarily to weight training, something few women were prepared to admit to in those days. As for stripping for God, one must read her books to get the full story.

312. Canadian magazine proprietor Robert Kennedy wanted to get in on the burgeoning popularity of women's exercise, so he began publishing *Bodybuilding for Women* in 1979. His first task was to convince women that weights would not make them muscle-bound monsters. Kennedy insisted that weight training was "the best method to shape the female body." Clearly, "bodybuilding" for women still meant "figure control," not muscle-building. A huge paradigm shift was destined to take place in just a year or two, and this magazine and others like it were preparing women for real physique building.

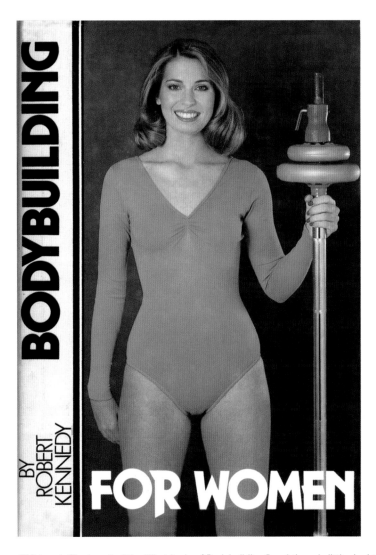

313 (*right*). She is called the "First Lady of Bodybuilding," and there is little doubt that Doris Barrilleaux (shown here c. 1978) was one of the first women to train for muscularity rather than "figure development." She sent a double-biceps pose of herself to *Strength and Health* magazine in 1962, but it was returned with a request for a more "feminine" picture. From there, Doris went on to organize women's bodybuilding competitions and to encourage other females to build their bodies with weights.

DORIS BARRILLEAUX AND JIM MURRAY

inside weight training for women

A comprehensive regimen tailored to condition the body and improve the figure of any woman—regardless of age or body type—without affecting the musculature of femininity

314. In 1978, Doris Barrilleaux founded the "Superior Physique Association" or S.P.A., which attempted to raise awareness of the women's bodybuilding movement. The first S.P.A. newsletters was sent out in September 1980. Barrilleaux was interested in promoting women's natural muscularity. She wanted to establish a new sport, not promote the usual girly figure models. The women bodybuilders on the cover of this issue are Cheryl Jones, Nancy Lytch, and Kelly Mitchell.

315. In addition to her other organizational tasks, Doris Barrilleaux was a tireless author of exercise and weight-training books for women. By 1978, when she co-wrote *Inside Weight Training for Women*, more and more females were willing to give barbell and dumbbell training a try. Her co-author, Jim Murray, was an editor at *Strength and Health* magazine; he had previously penned several exercise books for men.

316. In the mid-1970s to the early 1980s, women began to display their physiques in a totally different way than they had in the previous two decades. They were graceful and beautiful, but they were also unquestionably muscular. In this photograph from Doris Barrilleaux's *S.P.A. News* dated 1980, Jan Beitz has the temerity to flex her biceps in a way that had not been seen in decades.

317. Bodybuilder Jacqueline Nubret was married to French bodybuilder Serge Nubret, and although she was not particularly muscular, she did train regularly with weights. "It may seem paradoxical," she has written, "but pumping iron has given me my feminine curves and gracefulness." Her seeming amazement at the "feminizing" power of weight training in order to mold a woman's form illustrates the discovery, in the late 1970s and early '80s, that allowed women to cease exercising with brooms and beanbags and begin to work out with heavier weights.

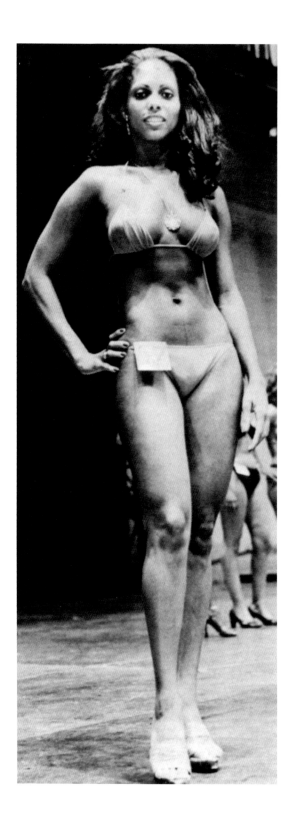

318. Jennifer Walters is a perfectly nice girl, but don't make her angry. She turns green and muscle-y and becomes the "Savage She-Hulk." Like her male counterpart, the She-Hulk represented a part of the psyche that was inappropriate to show in public. This comic book, which appeared in 1980, reflected the angry, powerful monster inside many externally compliant women. It was a perfect metaphor for the way lots of female physique athletes felt at the time.

CONCLUSION: LET'S GET PHYSICAL

The rapidly growing popularity of women's bodybuilding in the last decades of the twentieth century should not have come as a complete surprise to most observers, as the late 1970s and early '80s saw an unprecedented interest in female fitness. Many women began to spend increasing amounts of time and money on diets, workout routines, gym memberships, and exercise contraptions—all so that they could capture the evanescent glow of health and firm muscularity that was suddenly and inextricably linked to beauty. It seemed as if most North Americans wanted to put the riots, disruptions, and uncertainties of the Vietnam War, Watergate, and the turmoil of the 1960s and '70s behind them. The Age of Aquarius had morphed into the "Me Generation."

It wasn't as if the athletic revolution of the early 1980s had sprung up out of the blue, however; there were earlier precursors of the movement. In 1971, women's fitness pioneer Jacki Sorensen opened an aerobic dancing studio in the basement of a New Jersey church where she played peppy music in the background to keep everyone in step; thus "Jazzercise" was born. Richard Simmons, once an overweight child from New Orleans, transformed himself into a flamboyant exercise guru after opening a fitness studio in Beverly Hills in 1974. Five years later, in 1979, the most famous workout diva of all, Jane Fonda, opened her first gymnasium in Southern California. Thanks to the efforts of these and other leaders, millions of women (and a few men) exercised together in groups, doing leg lifts, side bends, and butt crunches, all to upbeat, bouncy disco music.

Aerobics and physical exercise made an incalculable impact on society in the

1980s. Muscles and jogging were in; flab and inactivity were out. Not even the anorexic world of fashion modeling could escape the fitness trend. Eileen Ford, owner of a top agency in New York, complained in a *Time* magazine article, "Models used to look fragile, plucking their eyebrows and wearing pancake makeup. God, they looked terrible! Now I get girls in here who are so fit they've got legs like [heavyweight boxing champion] Muhammad Ali." In the 1980s a youthful, slim (but not overly thin), fit, and suntanned body became synonymous with beauty. In the same *Time* article, Helen Gurley Brown, editor of *Cosmopolitan* magazine, declared that good health made women sexier. "Women are becoming real sexual athletes," she wrote. A strong body translated into a confident, attractive, and more sexually aggressive woman. Many men appeared to enjoy the new look, too. This was apparent when even the prostitutes who trolled for johns along Los Angeles's Sunset Strip wore tank tops, headbands, jogging shorts, and leg warmers while working. "Jock chic" had moved out of the fitness salon and into the streets.

Bodybuilding—real muscle building rather than figure control—was now a possibility for females who were so inclined. The Women's World Bodybuilding Championship was held at the Embassy Auditorium in Los Angeles in June of 1979; the winner was Lisa Lyon, a pretty and charismatic physique athlete who became something of an instant star. It was quickly apparent to the men's organizations that women would be a potent force in the athletic world, and that they had better adapt or lose a valuable franchise. Consequently, by 1980 there was a rapid and enthusiastic explosion of women's competitions. The Amateur Athletic Union (AAU), World Amateur Body Building Association (WABBA), National Amateur Body-Builders' Association (NABBA), World Body Building Guild (WBBG) and, most important of all for professional physique athletes, the International Federation of Body Building (IFBB) all formed women's competitions. In 1980, this last group organized the largest, most prestigious, and best-paying contest ever held, the Ms Olympia. The winner of that competition was Rachel McLish, the first in a long series of true female physique stars who have become famous for their muscularity.

It only took a couple of years after the advent of women's professional bodybuilding for the contestants to begin using male hormones and other anabolic steroids. These drugs brought about a dramatic new look to female physique athletes. To many, it meant that women began to look more and more muscular, thus more masculine. A heavily muscled female physique (built with devilishly hard work and more than a little pharmaceutical assistance) was now possible for the first time. This was a look that outraged many observers and caused some to turn away in disgust from the sight of an unrepentantly muscular woman who had built her body beyond the socially acceptable norms. Having a fit and taut physique was tolerated, even encouraged, but the overly muscular bodies that were possible after 1980 were something else entirely.

Controversies have continued to swirl around female bodybuilding. With the use of steroids and other pharmacological aids to muscle-building, women keep on pushing the definition of athleticism, gender, and muscularity. Unfortunately, the introduction of drugs has meant that, once again, many people regard female bodybuilders as freaks. How ironic it is that, even after 200 years, we still have not gotten used to the sight of a super-buff female. As they have for centuries, strong women can still cause us to be variously admiring, aroused, shocked, fearful, uncomfortable, and more than a little confused. Physically strong women have the power to move the goalposts of gender and beauty in a myriad of interesting directions.

JANE FONDA'S WORKOUT RECORD

With instructions by Jane Fonda.

Featuring the music of: The Jacksons REO Speedwagon Brothers Johnson Linda Clifford Billy Ocean Jimmy Buffett Boz Scaggs

319. Actress, feminist, and exercise maven Jane Fonda caught the aerobics bug late in the 1970s, taking it further than any other woman. Fonda opened her first exercise salon in 1979 and she soon discovered that if she used disco music and videotapes, she could widen her audience considerably. This record, featuring various pop rock and disco tunes, first appeared in 1981, but Fonda was by then already a familiar figure with her striped top and her muscular, leotard- and leg-warmer-encased legs sticking up, forming a V for victory over flab and inactivity.

320. The first Women's World Bodybuilding Championship was held in June of 1979; the victor was a charismatic athlete named Lisa Lyon. She was good in front of the cameras and soon became something of a media darling. The public had never seen a physique like hers before; she became the face and body of the new women's bodybuilding movement. "Before the advent of Lisa," wrote historian Al Thomas, "the women of the '70s who are committed to heavy training have not known what ideal to strive for." Now they knew.

321. There had been muscular women before Lisa Lyon—many of them, but they never really had the right combination of sexiness and muscularity to make them stars. Lisa was different. She had a thin, strong physique and knew how to show it off. Suddenly, female bodybuilding had a spokeswoman who looked different from the beauty queens who had previously populated the posing platforms of women's bodybuilding. She balanced her muscularity with her femininity, an intoxicating mixture for the general public. This exercise photo is from a 1980 feature article on Lyons in *Iron Man* magazine.

322. Although her image was a familiar one thanks to her appearance in many bodybuilding magazines, Lisa Lyons' most enduring legacy was photographer Robert Mapplethorpe's 1983 book, *Lady: Lisa Lyon*. Before that, she had appeared in *Playboy* and other publications. Ironically, Lyon competed only once and then quickly retired from bodybuilding.

323. There was still some confusion about how strong women should appear in photographs—seductive and attractive, or strong and muscular? Most female physique athletes, such as Kris Alexander (shown here in the early 1980s), opted for a combination of the two.

324. Other stars were starting to appear in the firmament of women's bodybuilding by the late 1970s. Carla Dunlap won the first Amateur Athletic Union Ms America contest in 1980, and she would later go on to greater heights. Dunlap and others like Patsy Chapman were among the first African-American women to succeed in the sport. As more contests opened up for muscular women, the more muscular the physiques became.

325. The most important professional bodybuilding organization in the world is the International Federation of Body Building (IFBB), founded in 1946 by Joe and Ben Weider, which saw the growing interest generated by women's bodybuilding in the 1970s. In 1980 the IFBB decided to hold its first contest for women, the Ms Olympia competition. This woman, Rachel McLish, was the winner of that contest, taking the sport to another level. Thanks to her unprecedented muscularity and electric posing abilities, McLish was in many ways the first modern female bodybuilder. Due to innovative muscle-building techniques and the newly available drugs with which women were experimenting, her vastly more muscular physique was unique for the time. McLish's physique marked a controversial but novel turning point for female muscularity. McLish offered a new and exciting direction for muscular women, but as we have seen, she is part of a venerable tradition of female strength that stretches back over two centuries.

A-plus Pears, 318–319
Abbenda, Joe, 322
aerobics, 347
Alaska, 206
Alberti, Leone Battista, 25
Alexander, Kris, 354–355
All-American Girls Professional Baseball
    League, 258–259
Amateur Athletic Union, 303, 355
American Venus, The, 206–207
Anna, the Physical Culture Girl, 82–83
Ansorge, Jean, 246
Anthonius, Anna, 107
Apollon Venus, 289
artists, 16, 25, 36–37
Athelda, 102–104
Athleta, 62–67
athletes, 15–16, 37–38, 58, 142–143, 154–155,
    197, 294
Attila, Louis, 122
Austria, 61

Baird, Gracie, 242
Banner, Lois, 31
Banta, Martha, 36
Baratini, Gloria, 265
Barbie doll, 39
Barker, Lex, 280
Barnum & Bailey Circus, 112. *See also*
    Ringling Brothers Circus
Barrilleaux, Doris, 341, 343–344
Bartky, Sandra Lee, 23
baseball, 258–259
bathing suits, 170–171, 194
Baumann, Caroline, 122
beauty, female, 28–29, 31–32, 35
Beauty and Health, 176–177
Beecher, Catharine, 30
Belgium, 65, 86, 331
Bellas, Bruce (photographer), 280–281
Belskie, Abram, 38
Blaikie, William, 36
body, female, 12, 14, 22–23, 26–29, 104, 196
body, male, 24, 27, 34
bodybuilding/bodybuilders, 7–9, 11–12,
    16, 18–19, 23, 34, 40, 234, 274–275, 286,
    293–294, 299, 340–345, 348–356
    associations, 348

Bodybuilding for Women, 340–341
Braselly Sisters, 115
Brewer, Relna, 7, 234
Bringing Up Father, 310–311
Brooks, Romaine, 36
Brown, Helen Gurley, 348
Brumbach, Katie, 32
Buffalo Bill, 82
Burke, Mildred, 260–261, 263
Byrrh, 161

Cahn, Susan, 37
California, 7, 22, 278, 282
Camel cigarettes, 254–255
Campell, Jack (artist), 256–257
Canada, 93
Cardonick, Deborah, 324–325
Cavett, Dick, 28
Chanel, Coco, 38
Chapman, Patsy, 355
Charles, Cecil (photographer), 266, 272–274
Charmion, 2, 33, 108
Chéret, Jules, 70–71
Chicago, 33
China, 25
Christensen, Vera, 324–327
circuses, 15, 17, 21, 32–33, 48, 53–54, 126,
    134, 268, 270–271
Clementinos Troupe, 78
Clias, Phokion H., 135
Collin Troupe, 122–123
comic books/strips, 10, 233, 250–251, 265,
    290–291, 310–314, 328–329, 336–337, 346
Comstock, Anthony, 35
Connell, Raewyn, 24
Corman, Roger, 338–339
Crawley, Pauline "Hedy", 258
Crocket, Vivian, 278–279
Cyr, Louis and Mélina, 93

Dairymaids, The, 118–121, 157
Dardenne, Georges and Monique, 331
Dickinson, Robert Latou, 38
Didrikson, Babe, 37–38, 197
Dior, Christian, 39
Dobbins, Bill, 23
Doublier, Madame, 54–55
Duboise, Madam, 90–91

Duke's Cigarettes, 146–147
Dunlap, Carla, 355
Dunphy, Charlotte, 147, 149
Dyer, Richard, 23

Ederle, Gertrude, 37
Edison, Thomas, 2, 33, 108
Ehrenreich, Barbara, 22
Eldred, Ethel, 172–173
Eliason, Marge, 284
Ella, Mildred, 197
Ella Cinders, 265
Elvgren, Gil (artist), 305
Emerson, Ralph Waldo, 29
England. *See* Great Britain
Estonia, 37
eugenics, 173
Europe, 16–17, 30, 51, 107, 122, 197
Everts, Kelli, 340
exercise, 12, 15, 17, 30, 48, 135–141, 150, 154,
    157–161, 183–184, 195, 199, 204–205, 224,
    227, 229, 321, 331, 347

Fabulous Moolah, 263–265
Farra, Marta, 132–133
fashion, 14, 29, 38–39, 196, 348
femininity, 16, 22, 37, 40, 48
feminism, 36, 294
Fierstein, Laurie, 9
Finland, 107
fitness, 12, 15, 48, 163, 347–348
Floria, Regina, 126
Folies Bergère, 82
Fonda, Jane, 347, 350
Ford, Eileen, 348
Fowler, Orson Squire, 26
France, 32, 54, 59, 67, 73, 80, 82, 85, 191, 212,
    227, 289, 308
Fried, Vera, 274
Friedan, Betty, 294

Galen, 25
Gay, Maureen, 322
gender identity, 22
Germany, 50, 62, 76–77, 79, 107, 126, 130,
    166–169, 187, 196, 218
Gillem, Gladys "Killem", 249
Gillot, Jeanne, 67–68

Gilman, Charlotte Perkins, 31, 36

Glasier, Frederick Whitman (photographer), 2, 108

Godey's Lady's Book, 30

Gold's Gym, 22

Grant, Vernon (artist), 255

Great Britain, 30, 32, 88, 97–98, 102, 117, 129, 151, 153, 229–230, 233, 251, 286

Greece, 25

Grimek, John, 242

Guerriere dal Seno Nudo, Le, 338

GutsMuths, Friedrich, 135

gymnastics, 142, 144–147, 153, 166, 204, 224, 227

Harmon, L.C., 151–152

Havana, 220–221

Headington, J.R., 12

Health and Life, 208–209

Health and Physical Culture, 220

Health & Strength, 98, 286–287

Hébert, Georges, 165, 191–193

Held, Jr., John (artist), 33

Heliot, Claire, 98

Herculine, Madame, 73

Hersey, George, 25, 27

Heywood, Leslie, 9, 40

Hodsdon, Gerry, 303

Hoffman, Bob, 237–238, 249, 323

Honeyman Heath, Barbara, 28

Hooton, Ernest, 27

Hope, Bob, 308

Illustrated London News, 153

International Federation of Body Building, 348, 356

Iron Man, 283, 300–302, 313, 328, 352

Italy, 224–225, 240–241

Jazzercise, 347

Jocher, Beverly, 294–295

Johnson, Lydia, 286

Jones, Cheryl, 342–343

Jowett, George, 208

Jumbo Comics, 251

Kellerman, Annette, 170, 194, 198

Kennedy, Robert, 340

Ketterman, Alda, 248–249

King, Billie Jean, 335

Klein, Sigmund, 234, 284

Klimunt, Amanda, 124

Kline, Richard, 228–229

Kretschmer, Ernst, 27

Kuriyama, Shigehisa, 25

Kyser, Kay, 234

La Blanche, Flossie, 60–61

La Milo, 117

Lady Wrestler, 322

Lala, Miss, 70–71

LaLanne, Jack, 8–9, 314–317

Lamour, Dorothy, 229

Langtry, Lillie, 32

Lanza, Tony (photographer), 283

Laspina, Gina, 294

Latvia, 215

Lawa, Stanil, 210–211

Leandros, the, 86–87

Lebensreform Bewegung. See Life Reform Movement

Leers, Luise, 104–107

Lehman, Dorcas, 234, 237–239

Leitzel, Lillian, 134, 208

Lewis, Diocletian, 135, 140–141

Liederman, Helmar, 206

Life Reform Movement, 218–220

Lombroso, Cesare, 27

Los Angeles, 7, 274, 303, 348

Lovequist, Evelyn, 298–299

Luftmann, Elise Serafin, 51

Lundini, 216

Lupino, Ida, 229

Lyon, Lisa, 40, 348, 350–353

Lytch, Nancy, 342–343

Macfadden, Bernarr, 13, 34–35, 40, 176, 179–180, 183, 187–188, 199–200, 232, 289

Maddux, Barbara, 22

Madison Square Garden, 13, 35, 179

Malaya, 226–227

Mansfield, Alan, 22

Mapplethorpe, Robert, 352

Marble, Alice, 197

Marguerite and Hanley, 88

Marseille, 69

masculinity, female, 37

Mathé, James, 308

McCracken, Elizabeth, 40

McCullah, Jackie, 278–279

McGhee, Henry, 294

McGinn, Barbara, 22–23

McLish, Rachel, 356

McRae, Relna, 268–269, 272–273

Mead, Margaret, 28

Meeker, "Dainty Marie", 208

Minerva, 33

Miss America, 206–207

Miss Bikini, 334–335

Miss Body Beautiful, 284

Miss Ella, 100–101

Miss Muscle Beach, 278–280, 282

Miss USA, 298–299

Miss World Body Beautiful, 323–325

Mitchell, Kelly, 342–343

Modern Physical Cult, 226–227

Mollerup, Paula, 328

Moore, Carrie, 118–121

Mr. America magazine, 332–333

Ms. magazine, 336

Ms. Marvel, 336–337

Ms. Olympia, 11, 348, 356

Mumford, Lewis, 37

Murray, Jim, 343

music hall, 47–48, 54

Muscle Beach, 7–8, 40, 266, 268, 272–273, 278–280, 282, 294–297

Muscles magazine, 330–331

Muscular Development, 40

Neser, L. and P., 130–131

New Museum of Contemporary Art, 9

New York, 7, 9, 13, 33, 122, 132–133, 277

New York Herald, 147–148

New York Illustrated News, 147–148

New York Standard, 56–57

Newkirk, Emma, 35

Njord, Val, 278, 280–281

Norm and Norma, 38–39

Nubret, Jacqueline and Serge, 344–345

O'Klady (artist), 290

Odell, Maude, 118–119

Otéro, Belle, 163

Parker, Kay, 283
Pearson, B.L. (photographer), 129
Penny Fiction, 58
Perlane, June, 130–131
Physical Culture, 13, 35, 159, 239, 288–289
photography/photographers, 16, 18, 28
physique contests, 11, 13
Picchiani, Luisa and Polissena, 121
Pinkham, Lydia, 187
Pissiuti, Esterina, 53
Plaston, Miss, 84
Plumaans, Lily, 331
PM Weekly, 234
Police Gazette, The, 16, 115, 142
Polykleitos, 25
Popard, Irène, 227
Power, Hiram, 26
Praxiteles, 25
Puck, 154
Pyechase, Penelope, 117

Redam, Ewald, 126–127
Reeves, Steve, 274, 277, 291–292
Rennie, Ron (photographer), 231–232
Rheinlander, Frances, 102
Rhodes, Joan, 308–309
Riebicke, Gerhard (photographer), 218
Riggs, Bobby, 335
Ringling Brothers Circus, 33, 107, 134
Rivers, Edna, 262, 274
Rivolta delle Gladiatrici, La, 338–339
Robert, Leo, 283, 300
Robert, Réjane, 283, 300–301, 313
Roberts, Kate, 94
Rockwell, Norman, 234
Romulo and Betty, 132
Rosie the Riveter, 234
Rouet, Marcel, 289–290
Rowan & Martin's Laugh-In, 332
Russell, Ivy, 229–231
Russell, Lillian, 32
Russia, 32

San Francisco, 151, 315
Sandow, Eugen, 33–34, 56–57, 116–118, 122, 187
Sandwina, 33, 110–115

Sansoni, Elvira, 98–101
Santa Monica, 7, 35, 266, 278
Sargent, Dudley Allen, 34–35, 38, 198
Savage She-Hulk, The, 346
Schiavoni Troupe, 100–101
Schwarzenegger, Arnold, 24, 294, 332–333
Scott, Barbara Ann, 37
Scrivens, Pat, 286–287
Secchi, Annette, 52–53
Semanya, Caster, 23
Sepisvort, Elvira, 80–81
sexuality, 37, 196
Sheena, Queen of the Jungle/Sheena, the Jungle Queen, 10, 233, 251, 336
Sheldon, William, 27–28
Simmons, Richard, 347
Smith, Evalynne, 242–243
Smith, Janel, 324–325
Society for the Suppression of Vice, 13
Sokol movement, 183
Sontag, Susan, 28
Sorensen, Jackie, 347
sports, 12, 17, 37–38, 195–196, 233
Sports Illustrated, 22
Stack, Mary Bagot, 197
Stage, Sarah, 31
Stanko, Steve, 242
steroids, 348–349
Stockton, Abbye "Pudgy", 7–8, 18, 40, 233, 262, 266–267, 272–277, 291–293, 325
Strength and Health/Strength & Health, 8, 233, 235, 237, 240, 246, 261, 267, 322–323. 325, 341, 343
Superior Physique Association/*S.P.A. News*, 342–344
Swedlund, Alan, 39

Tanny, Armand, 298–299
Tempest, Edna, 159, 183–184
Terret, Thierry, 212
Texie, 108–109
Thomas, Al, 13, 19, 350
Tigra the Werewoman, 336
Todd, Jan, 30, 230
Treloar, Al, 183
Turnverein, 166–167, 169

Unger, Paula, 7

United States Women's Physique Association, 294
Unus, Nina, 236–237
Urla, Jacqueline, 39

Vance, Bobbi, 323
vaudeville, 15, 17, 47–48, 62, 70, 130, 216
Venables, Gordon (illustrator), 235, 240
Verbrugge, Martha, 35
vinegar Valentines, 174–175
Voyce, Inez "Lefty", 258–259
Vulcana, 94–97

Waléry, Lucien, 82
Waters, Gladys, 247
Weed, C.L. (photographer), 90–91
Weider, Joe, 248, 356
weightlifting/weightlifters, 235, 237, 244, 246–248, 265, 267–269, 272, 274, 284–285, 297, 302–307, 319–321, 343
Welter, Barbara, 30
Wendt (photographer), 56
Wennerstrom, Steve, 294
West, Mae, 222–223
White, Willis T. (photographer), 157
Whitely Exerciser, 184–185
Winslow, "Chucky", 284–285
Wolf, Naomi, 28
Wolfram, Grete, 88–90
Women's Army Corps, 233, 252–253
Women's League of Health and Beauty, 197
Women's Physical Development, 176–177
Women's World Bodybuilding Championship, 348, 350–351
Wonder Woman, 233, 250–251, 290–291, 314, 328–329, 336
World War I, 38, 195, 233
World War II, 38, 233–234, 252–257
Worth, Charles, 32
wrestling/wrestlers, 47, 61, 107, 249, 260–261, 263–265, 322

Yarick, Alyce, 302
Your Physique, 280–281

Ziegfeld, Jr., Florenz, 33
Zygowicz, Loretta, 244–245

DAVID L. CHAPMAN is the author of twelve books on male photography and bodybuilding, including *American Hunks* (Arsenal, 2009), *Comin' at Ya!: The Homoerotic 3D Photographs of Denny Denfield* (Arsenal, 2007), *Adonis: The Male Physique Pin-up,* and two other books on Denny Denfield. He lives in Seattle.

PATRICIA VERTINSKY is a professor at the School of Human Kinetics at the University of British Columbia, specializing in the social and cultural history of the body. She is the author or editor of four previous books on sports and gender. She lives in Vancouver.